THUNDER from HEAVEN

From Gutter to Glory

DALE HOCH

THUNDER FROM HEAVEN
Copyright © 2016 by Dale Hoch

All rights reserved. Neither this publication nor any part of this publication may be reproduced or transmitted in any form or by any means, electronic or mechanical, including photocopying, recording or any information storage and retrieval system, without permission in writing from the author.

Scripture taken from the Holy Bible, King James Version, which is in the public domain.

Printed in Canada

ISBN: 978-1-4866-1140-9

Word Alive Press
131 Cordite Road, Winnipeg, MB R3W 1S1
www.wordalivepress.ca

Cataloguing in Publication information may be obtained through Library and Archives Canada.

Acknowledgements	v
Preface	vii

1: **HOW DID I GET HERE?**	1
2: **IN TROUBLE WITH THE LAW**	7
3: **GANG WARS, GUNS AND GOD**	13
4: **BURYING OUR BROTHERS**	25
5: **DESCENDING INTO THE DARKNESS**	33
PICTURES	53
6: **THE ROAD HOME**	59
7: **A SUPERNATURAL ENCOUNTER**	69
8: **MY BROTHER AND MY MOTHER**	85
9: **APPOINTMENTS FROM ABOVE**	95
10: **THE CALL**	105
11: **THE MESSAGE**	111

Acknowledgements

I want to thank my family, especially my wife Edith, for her support and love in the writing of this book. I would also like to say a personal word of thanks to word alive press staff and associates for all their great work in completion of this book.

I would also like to say a special thank you to Pastor JoAnne Danso, for the many hours she put into prayerfully typing this book. Also thanks to my brother Mac for his part. Special thanks to Mildred Schneider, who proofread the manuscript and encouraged me to publish this book.

It is not my intent to be derogatory against any person or to make accusations to harm anyone. This is simply the story of my life and some of the unfortunate circumstances of those who lived a similar lifestyle. The people I rode with in the Henchmen were my friends and colleagues. Even though we got into a lot of trouble, drank, partied, did drugs, and rode our motorcycles hard, we were still human beings. Every one of us had feelings; some were married, some had children, and some had full-time jobs. The Henchmen Motorcycle Club with which I was a member was not associated with any other club with the name Henchmen. It was solely a regional club. This book is simply meant to express that no matter how far a person sinks into a pit of despair and sin, you will never sink too far for the loving grace of God to pull you out.

Preface

Jesus came to die so that sinners might live. Jesus said, *"I am not come to call the righteous, but sinners to repentance"* (Matthew 9:13). The Bible says that all have sinned and fallen short of the glory of God. Jesus was really saying that everyone in the world needs a Saviour. I definitely do not want to glorify sin or make people think that sin is exciting. Sin is very destructive and has ruined many young people's lives. I've lost some very close friends, seen many go to prison, and watched lives torn apart by the ugliness of what sin can do to an individual. This book is a warning to young and old alike who are being tempted to go down that destructive road. Satan is not out to take any hostages. He is out to steal, kill, and destroy. Until he ultimately destroys people; Satan is never satisfied. The Bible says, *"There is a way which seemeth right unto a man, but the end thereof are the ways of death"* (Proverbs 14:12).

In my younger years, my life was basically a journey to hell and back, but I now fully understand grace and mercy.

For by grace are ye saved through faith; and that not of yourselves: it is the gift of God: not of works, lest any man should boast. (Ephesians 2:8–9)

Jesus said that those who *"believe in thine heart that God hath raised him from the dead, thou shalt be saved"* (Romans 10:9). I am a sinner who is saved by grace (undeserved favour).

I will never deserve to go to heaven, but I know that I'm going. Not because I'm good or better than anybody else, not because I'm a preacher, not because I've done good things for Jesus, but simply because I believe on Him who died for me, so I could have eternal life. Today, if you will believe on the Lord Jesus Christ and invite Him into your heart as your Lord and Saviour, you will have eternal life. God is more willing to forgive us than we are to receive His forgiveness. You can know that you are going to heaven through faith alone, as God declares in His Word (1 John 5:13).

I pray that as you read this book, you will open your heart and allow Christ to save you from your sin. Hopefully this story may stop someone from going down the same road of destruction I went down, or rescue someone who is currently on that same road. God can use you for His glory before you draw your last breath on this side of heaven and open your eyes on the other side with the Lord.

Finally, I would like to say that I love each and every one of the young men and women I was associated with during my years in the Henchmen. I hurt for many of them today, as they still have not become Christians. I respect each one of them, and I long to see them all in heaven. I have changed their names and nicknames in order to protect their privacy. This book is about my life and my encounter with the Lord who thunders from heaven.

As author of this book, I would like to share that I am now the full-time pastor of World Outreach Ministries, a church my wife Edith and I founded. The proper pronunciation of my name is Hoke, like the soft drink Coke; my nickname in the club, Hochie, is pronounced Hokie.

Chapter 1

HOW DID I GET HERE?

I never dreamed it possible that the day we thundered into a city in northern Ontario, my life would take a turn. I had no idea that the thunder of God rolled in with us.

I found myself in the middle of a field, all alone and lost. Not far from me I heard the sounds of bike gang members and their girlfriends. The Henchmen Motorcycle Club out of Kitchener was meeting with the Coffin Wheelers for a drunken bash flowing with illegal drugs and booze. We were at the farmhouse belonging to one of the guys from the rival club. I was heavily intoxicated with liquor, beer, and chemicals coursing through my body and mind. I had entered a realm of satanic hallucinations I thought I would never survive. Flames of hell exploded before me and I saw demonic faces and forces coming at me from every side. Feeling the horrors of a lost eternity, the outer darkness, the weeping and wailing, the screaming and gnashing of teeth, I stood on the very edge of hell. I felt like I was dying and being hurled into a hellish abyss with no hope. This happened at a point in my life when I was tired of living, yet I was afraid to die. I had already lost a number of close friends and attended far too many biker funerals.

That night, the powers of hell and darkness struggled to take my life at a very young age. I was drinking alcohol and electric wine (wine mixed with drugs) and eating drugs like candy for most of the day. I was dying from an overdose of drugs in my body; it was enough to have killed an elephant. Yet somehow I was still alive. I didn't know where to go, what to do, or who to talk to for help. I felt like I wouldn't live much longer if I didn't do something. Suicidal thoughts and tendencies ran through my mind. If only I could find a rope and hang it over the limb of a tree, it would all be over. I could end the torment. Satan has told that lie to millions of people who feel there is no way out.

Yet somehow I sensed that God was in that field with me, something I couldn't understand. It was as if there was a supernatural thunder in the distance: God coming to rescue me from the brink of destruction.

From my childhood, I knew there was a God somewhere in the universe. I was sent to Sunday school every week by my parents, who eventually became alcoholics. I knew there was a God I had to meet when I crossed over to eternity. I had believed this God was angry with me and that He hated me and would never forgive me for the things I had done. I always thought that if you lived a life filled with violence, drugs, criminal activity, and immoral behaviour, God would never allow you into heaven. As I stood in that field battling demonic forces, I felt that Lucifer himself came to deal with me for the things I had done wrong, the laws I had broken, and the crimes I had committed. I felt that I was now paying the price. None of the gang members at the farmhouse cared that I was literally dying in this field alone. They were too busy partying and taking their own cocktail of drugs and alcohol.

How did I end up in such a miserable, wretched position? Was there any way out? Was there a God out there who would care enough about me to help me out of this mess?

I was raised in a fairly normal home in a village called Heidelberg, just a few kilometres outside of Kitchener-Waterloo, fairly large cities situated in the centre of southwestern Ontario. My father helped manage a large store by the name of Highway Market, while my mother stayed home in the village to help raise us children. I have fond memories of a good life as a little boy. My parents were average people, we went to the village school, and my dad sent us to church on Sundays. He himself would never attend, but Mom always came along with us.

As children, we had a good life. Dad was a good provider and we always had food, good clothing, and some of the extras. My dad bought a new car every couple of years, and we even had a boat. As a little boy growing up in a small village, life seemed like it was going to be great. I could hardly wait to experience the splendours of tomorrow.

However, things began to change drastically when my mom and dad began to drink heavily. Alcoholism became the earmark of my dad's life. There was fighting and swearing, and Mom and Dad seemed to be constantly angry with each other. My father was a stern man, but my mother seemed to have the heart of an angel. Even though she would fight with my father, she still had a soft side, a tenderness that is hard to explain; it could only be experienced by living with this precious woman. If I ever experienced unconditional love, it was from my mother.

At school I began to have a rough time. My brother and sister were always getting better grades than me. I seemed to be the dunce of the family. I was a daydreamer and had no interest in school. I was always getting low marks. Mom and Dad told me that I had to do better in school. Dad said that if I didn't learn, I wouldn't amount to anything.

I continued to acquire failing grades and eventually ended up in remedial classes in special schools. I had longed to be smart like my brother and sister, who seemed to learn easily, but to me it was a constant battle. I also began to have problems with some of the other children in school, especially with the boys who were known as bullies. The bigger, older boys would pick on me and laugh at me; they called me "baby-face Hoch."

One day, they asked me to go into the washroom with them. I thought maybe they were going to let me be part of their group; finally, I could be one of the boys. I would then be somebody, because at the time I felt like a nobody. As soon as I walked in, one of the bigger boys punched me in the mouth and knocked me down. They all walked out laughing and left me there alone. I became very sad and angry.

Not only did I feel dumb, I felt like a coward, because I would run away from fights. I would run away and hide rather than be punched again. I was ashamed of myself. A bully at school always wanted to fight me, but I was terrified. I told him I would meet him to fight on the last day of school out in the yard. When that day came, I slipped out the side door and ran all the way home.

When I was only eight years old, I saw motorcycle gangs in the area. We had a huge hill not far from our house called Mount Coone, and motorcycle riders from all over Canada and the United States would come to race up it. They would gain a trophy for their efforts. At the time, I was too young to go out to the hill climb and watch these powerful motorcycles compete. However, I was impressed with motorcycles and those tough men who rode them, especially the gang members.

This event attracted hundreds of bikers, but it also attracted bike gangs from across Canada and the United States. There was Satan's Choice, Lobos, Queen's Men, Paradise Riders, Vagabonds, Red Devils, Grim Reapers, and Wild Ones, just to name a few. These gangs came to terrorize our little town. I remember standing on the front porch of our home and watching as the bikes rolled in by the hundreds. They would race up and down in front of our house with screaming tires and loud blaring pipes. I watched as they thundered into town, laughing and screaming with wild girls on the back of their bikes. They wore leather jackets, chains, heavy motorcycle boots, and their hair streamed in the wind (these were the days before helmets were required by law).

These gang members would literally take over our town for an entire day. The people would talk about them for weeks after they left. I would hear stories about them dancing on tables at the hotel, breaking chairs and fighting. I watched as they kicked in car doors. Police cars came screaming in from every direction with their sirens wailing and lights flashing. The police would try and load these bike gang members into patty wagons. While they were cramming them in, the bikers would rock the vehicle from side to side. There was fighting on the streets and at the hill climb. Alcohol and drugs were always present.

Somehow, I began to admire the lifestyle. I realized that people were afraid of them and would talk about them for a long time. I thought to myself, *Here are the nobodies of society, and they've become somebodies.* They did it in the wrong way, but they were recognized by society. They weren't just faces in the crowd, people to be pushed around and punched out. They were tough and feared! They didn't care what anybody thought or said about them. They wore their colours on their back and were proud to display what they believed. They were showing people what they stood for, and they put their lives on the line.

If only people would take that kind of fearless stand for Jesus, this world would be a different place.

When I was a little older, I got a chance to actually go to the hill climb. I watched as gang members took out knives and threatened those from rival clubs. Any gang member found alone, was fair game and prey to the others. I watched as tougher guys from one gang took out knives and cut the crests off the back of jackets from rival clubs. These were souvenirs to take back to their clubhouse and hang on the wall. They had to show that they were the tougher, meaner gang, and this was a sign that they had conquered the weaker guy. This would usually incite gang and turf wars between rival clubs. The rule was death before dishonour; nobody was allowed to take your patch.

I longed to one day become a bike gang member. I didn't care what it cost me. I believed that if I could ride a motorcycle and wear a club crest on my back, people would know and respect me. I wouldn't be pushed around, laughed at, or made fun of any more. People would fear me and I would have a name.

At the age of eight, I set my heart on one day becoming one of the men I considered my heroes. I didn't realize the destructive path it would take me down and what a horrible end it would bring to some of my friends' lives.

When I was ten years old and we moved to Kitchener, the trauma of moving from a village school to a city school was very difficult for me. I failed my grades that year while my brother and sister progressed. I was kept back a year and made me feel even more like a failure. A year after that, I was sent to a special remedial school, separated from my brother and sister because the teachers said I couldn't learn. I had a learning disability, and therefore I needed special teaching. This was humiliating for me, and I cried out inside my heart: *Why do I have to be so dumb? Why am I such a nothing?* I longed to make something more of myself. I began to look in all the wrong places, trying to find that type of life.

Dad's alcoholism got the best of him over the next couple of years. Before I reached my teen years, we lost the house and my dad lost his job. We were forced to move to the inner city and buy an older home. We were able to acquire a small variety store and tried to make ends meet by selling groceries. However, with both of my parents drinking heavily, they went bankrupt and we lost almost everything.

Sometimes at Christmas, Dad was so drunk that he wouldn't let us open our gifts. We would cry out to Mom, but there was nothing she could do; Dad ruled the household, and what he said had to be obeyed.

He ended up in jail one night after becoming violent. He eventually ended up in a hospital in London, Ontario. When he was released, my parents joined Alcoholics Anonymous and were finally able to break the demonic hold of alcoholism on their lives. They weren't Christians, but they always said they believed in God.

I really do believe that Dad loved us, but he was never able to express that in words, nor were we able to say that we loved him. The word love was never used around our house. My precious mother suffered a lot through those years, and there was no doubt in our minds that she loved all of us dearly. She sacrificed so much to try and give us a better life. She worked hard in a factory trying to bring home enough money to pay the bills.

Chapter 2

IN TROUBLE WITH THE LAW

My sixteenth birthday was a milestone in my life. I felt like I had new freedom; I could get my license, I could buy a car, and finally I could do the things I wanted to do in life. I acquired a job with a landscaping company and was able to save enough money to buy an old 1954 Pontiac. To me, it was the most beautiful car in the world, just as good as having a brand new vehicle. The one thing I didn't like about the car was that it had a pink-peach colour. Nonetheless, I had a car that I could drive and enjoy life.

I had done some part-time work at a supermarket on Highland Road in Kitchener, and there I met a young man who took me down a road I had always dreamed about—being part of a gang. He used to hang around with a street crowd known as Dell's Angels. The guys used to hang out and party at their houses, occasionally getting into some trouble. They were becoming a household name for some people in our city due to their wild parties, fighting, and criminal activities.

One night, this same young man, who wore a leather jacket, asked me to join him and the other guys. They were going down to a garage to hang out for a little while. I gladly accepted, believing this was my big break, my hour to shine. I met some of the group that night as we sat around the garage drinking beer and straight liquor. I had never drunk straight liquor in my life. I didn't tell any of the guys that evening that I was a novice drinker. Even though my parents were alcoholics, I tended to stay away from alcohol, largely due to the iron-fist control my dad had over me. I would drink the liquor, pretending to be tough, and then go outside privately and get sick. I didn't want to be a spectacle in front of my new friends. Nor did I want them to think I couldn't handle the booze.

After a few nights of hanging out and drinking, I began to get used to the liquor. Some nights I staggered home drunk, falling down on the sidewalk because of the large amounts of alcohol I was consuming.

One particular evening, one of the guys started talking about breaking into a school. He said that he knew how to get into the principal's office, where we'd find all kinds of neat stuff we could steal and sell. Some of the others thought it was a great idea. They were all for it, so they began planning a break and enter. I remember thinking to myself, *Boy, I want to be part of this gang and I want to drink and party with them, but I don't want to break into a school.* I was pretending to be tough on the outside, but on the inside I was still a coward.

I was a hypocrite, pretending to be something I really feared. There are hypocrites in every walk of life—in the halls of government, in our schools, in our police forces. In model homes and model families, people are pretending. They are living a lie. Some people say that hypocrites are only found in churches, but I beg to differ.

I've found that some of the biggest hypocrites in life are the guys and girls I hung around with in the club. They were also pretending to be something when they were nothing. They would betray each other and steal behind each other's backs.

One of the guys finally looked over at me and said, "Hey Hochie, do you have what it takes to break into a school, or are you afraid?"

Terrified, I wanted to say, "I don't want to get involved with that. I don't want to get in trouble with the police and get arrested." I wanted to be part of the gang and have fun, but I didn't want to get into that kind of trouble.

You can't hang out with the devil and live the life of an angel. One thing I have learned is that sin will take you further than you want to go, it will keep you longer than you want to stay, and it will make you do things you never thought you would do.

Despite my fears and doubts, I snapped back at him, "I'm not afraid." I was lying through my teeth. "I'll go along with you guys and I'll bust into that school, and I'll show you how it's done."

They all laughed as they continued to plan the break-in.

The next weekend, as we approached the school, we went around back where nobody could see what we were doing. We took out our tools and began to take the hinges off one of the back doors. After the door came loose, we were able to squeeze in.

We walked down the hallways of the school. In those early years, schools didn't have alarm systems, so we weren't afraid that the police would be alerted to a silent signal.

We made our way to the principal's office and broke in. We stole some tape recorders and stopwatches. In one of the drawers we found a starter's pistol; it was used for track and field and it only shot blanks, but to me it was a prized possession. It looked like a real gun.

After half an hour of wandering through the school and stealing a bunch of stuff, we finally left with our bags full of loot. We got away without anybody knowing. Nobody had seen us or caught us in the act. I began to grow a little braver.

Sin will eventually make your conscience grow cold and indifferent. The next weekend, we broke into a laundromat and broke open the machines to steal the money. One night we broke into a hospital cafeteria. Then we began to break into more schools.

This went on for months. The fear of being caught no longer bothered me. I had become accustomed to this lifestyle. I began to enjoy breaking into these facilities and receiving the gains of a criminal life. The one thing I forgot is that your sins will always find you out, according to Numbers 32:23. Sooner or later, you'll pay the price. Sooner or later, somebody is going to catch you and you're going to pay for the things you've done wrong.

One dark night, we broke into the back of another high school. While taking off the back door, I had a strange feeling that something wasn't right. I walked out to the corner of the building to look around and saw a police cruiser driving in with his lights turned off. I then looked up into the windows of the school. One of the caretakers was in the window looking out at us. He had been camped out there overnight, because there had been so many break-ins at city schools. He'd phoned the police when he heard us banging on the back door.

I yelled to the other guys, "The cops!" They all dropped their tools and ran out into the field behind the school.

As we were running in different directions, lights came on from different sides of the schoolyard. The police had already surrounded the place. I remember hearing a policeman yell, "Stop or I'll shoot." It was the first time I ever saw a policeman's gun outside of its holster—and it was pointed in my direction. I stopped and threw up my hands. As the police approached, they handcuffed my hands behind my back and frisked me. None of us got away that evening.

We were taken down to the police station, which I had only ever seen from the outside, and booked with break and entry and theft. I was sixteen years old at the time. We were taken to an area with cells, creating fear and uncertainty in my mind.

Just beyond those cells were interrogation rooms. Each one of us was put into a different room, and for the next three hours they interrogated us separately. They wanted to find out how many break-ins we had committed over the last few months. Because nobody knew what the others were saying, the police were able to figure out when we were lying.

The police used us against each other. I recall the detective saying that one of the other guys had confessed to different crimes, so I might as well confess also. It was a psychological tactic that I didn't understand at the time. The other guys may have said nothing. Once someone finally confessed, they charged us with numerous break and entries and thefts.

After the interrogation, the police loaded me into a cruiser and drove me home. While most members in the gang were older than me, that particular night I was hanging with guys who were juveniles. They were only fifteen years old, but I was sixteen. I was at the age where I was considered an adult and could acquire a permanent criminal record. The police took me to the front door of our house and my dad answered. They explained to him that I had been caught with a group of boys committing a break and entry and that we had also committed other crimes. They told him that I was being charged, but that they wouldn't lock me up for the night because it was my first offence.

I walked into the front hall that night, my dad looking angry and my mom looking sad. Dad said to me, "Dale, you've made your own bed and now you're going to have to lie in it."

I felt ashamed and guilty. I felt like a big failure again. It seemed like no matter what I did, it always ended up the same way: in a hopeless situation.

I was grounded and went through a fairly difficult period the next year. The other boys and I went to court and were arraigned on the charges. The judge gave me a suspended sentence and put me on two years of probation. He told me that I wasn't allowed to hang out with the Dell's Angels.

I stayed out of trouble for a couple of years and my life took on a fairly normal atmosphere. My brother and I purchased hot cars. It was the thing all young people were doing at the time. I began to hang out with a set of new friends, going to parties and having fun. We would go to the A&W drive-in and squeal our tires, just having a good time.

Not long after my court case, I got a phone call at work. I was told that something had happened to my father and I needed to get home immediately. When I arrived at the house, my brother looked dazed and my sister and mom were crying. They told me that dad had had a massive heart attack and that he had died instantly. We never had a chance to say goodbye or spend some final moments with him.

I remember going to his funeral and looking into the coffin. I shed a tear and said in my heart, *Dad, could you come back just for ten minutes? Could you just give me a little time so that I could tell you that I love you?*

I never did tell my dad that I loved him. How I have always regretted that, and how I wish that my dad and I would have expressed our true feelings for each other. I always tell young people, let your parents know that you love them now while they're still alive. Don't wait until you're putting them in the ground. Parents also need to express love for their children, because you never know what life may bring their way!

After my dad died, my mom was forced to take in boarders to make ends meet. Life was a struggle financially, but I knew my mom really loved and cared for us. I had the kind of mother who always did without things for herself so she could provide for her family.

Somehow we made it through even though my mother seemed to always be on the edge of poverty. Yet she seemed to pay the bills, put food on the table, and always have a place for us to sleep. We had some really good times during those years. We were always able to bring our friends to the house. My mother was of the opinion that it was better that we be at home under her supervision than get into trouble on the streets. She was always very protective of us, but that didn't stop us from doing the sort of crazy things young people are inclined to do. There were the car races in the country, drinking on the back roads, and on it went.

Chapter 3

GANG WARS, GUNS, AND GOD

I tried to stay out of trouble after my run-in with the police in the break and entries. Still, deep inside me was a restlessness, a longing to be part of a group again. I needed to be part of a club that would make me feel like I had some worth and value in life.

After my father's death, I had no more manly influence to keep me restrained. I believe that was one of the major reasons I made so many bad decisions. A lot of young people today lack a father figure. They especially lack fathers who love the Lord and are the spiritual head of the home. Some parents don't show any love and affection, nor do they serve the Lord. They don't raise their families as Christians, so many young people rebel and go to the wrong places looking for things only God can give them. This is one of the greatest downfalls of our nation today with families. Proverbs 22:6 say, *"Train up a child in the way he should go; and when he is old, he will not depart from it."* They may drift for a season, but with prayer and love they will come back to their faith.

One day after coming home from work, I walked into the dining room of our house and saw a newspaper sitting on the table. I picked it up and looked at the bold headlines: "Three KW men gunned down in cycle club battle." As I read the article, something began to take hold of me in such a way that I had never felt before. The article said that there had been a shootout the night before on St. Ledger's Street in Kitchener, between the Henchmen Motorcycle Club and the Chosen Few, a rival gang in our city. Three people had been shot. One young man had forty-five shotgun pellets dug out of his back. Another young man was just an innocent bystander and got caught in the crossfire and was in the hospital on the critical list. The article said that six members of the Henchmen had been arrested and charged with attempted murder, as well as a number of the Chosen Few. The police said if the person who was critical died as a result of his wounds, they would raise the charges to murder.

The Henchmen were gaining quite a reputation for violence and were known as one of the most notorious clubs in all of Canada. One judge, with some Henchmen before him, said that their motorcycle club made Hitler's youth movement look like a bunch of choir boys.

After I finished reading the article, a power began to grip my mind and life. I know now that it was not the power of God; it was definitely demonic. If you believe there is a God in heaven, you also need to believe that there is a devil in hell. You need to understand that if there are angels that do warfare on behalf of the Lord Jesus Christ, there are also demons that do warfare on behalf of Lucifer. I believe those demons began to lie to me and take hold of my life. There are powerful forces today that are dragging young people into the occult, Satanism, gangs, and into massive drug abuse. Those forces are causing them to take weapons to school to shoot and kill their friends. Powers of demonic darkness are dragging young people into the most sordid behaviours that have ever been recorded on the face of planet earth.

This satanic power began to grip and control me that day. Reading that article should have been repulsive. It should have made me cringe and made me want to turn away from the people who belonged to such a gang. But I heard a voice whispering to me, "This is the kind of club you want to ride with. If you were a member of the Henchmen, you would be something. People would be afraid of you, young people would look up to you, and you would never be pushed around again."

I didn't care what it cost me or what I had to do. I made my decision the day I read that article. I was going to join this club.

I didn't know any of its members, but I did know a couple of people who were acquaintances of some of the Henchmen. When I told one young man that I wanted to join the club, he somehow passed word on to one of the gang members. One day I met that member in a hotel and he said to me, "I understand that you would like to come and join the club." I responded with a yes, and he said that he would sponsor me. To join a motorcycle gang, you had to have a sponsor who would back you up.

Then you had to go through a striking period that could last anywhere from a few months to a year or more. It depended on whether or not the club members liked you. This also determined how difficult they made it for a new member to join. At the time I was sponsored, a lot of the Henchmen were in hiding due to the heat from the police over the shootout a couple of weeks before. Some members were in jail. This meant that my striking period wasn't too difficult for the first little while. The most difficult thing I had to do was being forced into some petty criminal activity. One night I was over at someone's house where some of the members were drinking liquor, wine, and beer. I was forced to chugalug cheap wine until I couldn't drink anymore.

I drank for two hours straight. I had so much wine in me that I could hardly see where I was going. At the time, I owned a 650 Triumph Bonneville which I tried to ride to a restaurant. I staggered out of that house, got on my motorcycle, and rode through town drunk out of my head. I vaguely recall weaving from the white line to the curb, back and forth. It's amazing that I wasn't killed that night, because I was actually delusional. A couple of the other members followed behind me on their bikes.

We pulled up to a place known as Jimmy's Lunch on Victoria Street. We went in to have a coffee and a sandwich. I staggered into the door, felt sick, and went to the washroom. One of the other club members came into the washroom behind me. As he walked in, I saw a black hand full of warts coming out of the towel rack and going for his neck. I remember shoving him out of the way and saying, "Look out!" I didn't realize it at the time, but I'd had so much to drink that I was having alcoholic hallucinations.

It seemed that most of the members liked me and thought I would be an asset to their club. Before I struck, I had been riding with some friends who weren't part of any gang but just enjoyed to ride and have fun. My brother also bought a motorcycle and rode with us before I joined the Henchmen. I tried many times to talk my brother and other friends into joining the club. I didn't realize the price I would pay for making that decision. I was trying to drag them into a lifestyle I would eventually regret.

I will never forget the day I received my crest. It made me proud but changed me for the rest of my life, and not in a good way. We were at an outdoor bike meeting, gathering for a bike run up to a nearby beach. I desperately wanted to have my colours for that run. I asked the club president and the person who had sponsored me if they would consider initiating me and give me my crest for that run. That was the day I got my patch. They gave me one that had already been on the vest of another member. I think it belonged to a member they considered a rat for putting some other members in prison. It eventually became part of my responsibility to try and get this guy to even the score. As I put that patch on my back, I felt a sense of power and acceptance. I felt that I had become someone. It was a feeling of importance and superiority.

A sense of pride began to overwhelm me. The Bible says, *"Pride goeth before destruction, and an haughty spirit before a fall"* (Proverbs 16:18). That's exactly the kind of feeling that overwhelmed me—a worldly, arrogant pride, a haughty spirit that bike gang members know all too well, because of the fear society has for them.

I had a wild time the weekend of my first run up to the beach. We rented a cottage under the pretence of a married couple. Usually one of our members would dress up half-decent and get one of the girls of the club to go rent a cottage with him. They would tell the owner that they were married and that they wanted to have a quiet weekend together. After the cottage was rented, the entire gang would roll in and take it over for the weekend. Usually the owners were too scared to phone the police. If they challenged the club and tried to remove them from the property, they were threatened. Seldom did the owners press the bike members to vacate. Many times there was damage due to drunken brawls and malicious activity. That particular weekend saw a drive-by shooting. Somebody heard the bang. I was intoxicated that night and lying next to my motorcycle on the ground. We don't know who or why they fired the gun at us, but it was a shotgun because its pellets were found embedded in the side of the house and in the signs on the road. Nobody was hit or hurt, and nobody ever found out who fired that weapon.

A little later that weekend, we heard that one of the members got into an argument with some university students. We all travelled a couple of blocks to their nearby cottage, where a fight broke out. As one of the junior members of the club, I was required to stay in the middle of the fight whether I wanted to be there or not.

One young man came flying through the screen doors and out onto the lawn. After the fight was over, we returned to our cottage to assess the night's activities. One of the junior members striking at the same time as me had been seen running away from the fight. This angered the Henchmen, as the club believed in *all for one and one for all*. Nobody was ever allowed to back down or run away from a fight. They put that young member in the middle of the circle and each Henchman took turns punching and kicking him. The entire club that night beat that young man and warned him never to run from a fight again. That was the last time he ever ran away from anything. That beating actually caused him to become what they considered a good member, but what society would consider a hardened young man.

After joining the Henchmen, I began to make some newspaper headlines of my own. I was involved in different hotel brawls and arrested for certain violent crimes. On one of the more memorable nights, I was driving home from a hotel with a young member we called Banger. He was one of the bigger fellows and was very strong. We were pulled over by the police. Because it was in the late fall, we didn't have our motorcycles; we were riding in an automobile. They told us to get out of the car and began to check us for impaired driving and warrants. Banger was really upset with the policeman's attitude and he began to fight with him. The policeman wanted to throw Banger to the ground and handcuff him, but he overpowered the policeman and flung him over the hood of the cruiser. A second policeman, a rookie on the force, jumped into the police cruiser and began to scream frantically into the microphone for help.

While I was trying to deal with the situation with Banger and that policeman, cruisers came from every corner of the city. There must have been at least ten cruisers arriving within two minutes. Policemen ran toward us from every direction. As one policeman wrestled with me, trying to take me down, I saw Banger still wrestling with the other policeman over the hood of the cruiser, and two more on his back trying to pull him off. Three policemen weren't able to take this young man down, because he was so big. They finally did pull him to the ground and subdued, handcuffed, and arrested us.

To make things even worse, another car load of Henchmen had pulled up, which just added to the mêlée. I must admit that the police showed great restraint that night. Had it been another city in another country, we probably would have been shot. Throughout that half-hour event, there were approximately eight Henchmen present and fifteen to twenty policemen.

A few of us were arrested and taken to the police station. I was one of the first ones taken into the basement. I recall standing at the bottom of the stairs and watching four police officers carry Banger down the stairwell bodily. When they got to the landing, they rammed his head into the wall just like a battering ram, almost knocking him unconscious. They proceeded to beat him until his face swelled black and blue. After they finished with him, they took us all to separate cells, stripped us of our clothing, took away our blankets, and had us lay in the barren jail all night. They opened windows in that area of the prison so the cold fall air would blow in, causing us to shiver throughout the evening.

One of our lawyers was called in by some of the other members. This particular lawyer would drink, do drugs, and party with us at the clubhouse. When he came to the police station, he saw that we had no clothes and that we were freezing. He demanded that out clothes be given back to us or he would have the police officers in court. They assured him that they would return our clothes, and with that he went home to bed. The policemen kept their word and brought our clothes back to the cells. The only problem was that they had soaked our clothes in a tub full of water. It was impossible to put them on because it would only have caused us to be colder. We were charged with police assault and assault causing bodily harm, even though we also received a beating from the police.

I must say that I have a high respect for police officers, and many of them have become personal friends of mine. They have a tough job, and the majority of them do great work under very difficult circumstances. However, there were a few who took the law into their own hands and tried to mete out punishment for the abuse we hurled at them.

After being released from jail, it was just a continual life of riding, partying, drinking, and doing drugs. My brother and his friends had so far resisted joining up with the Henchmen, but one day, at the persuasion of another member, they decided to join. Not only was I going down a road to destruction, I was taking my family and friends with me.

One time, we partied with a club in Calgary. Most of the members drove out in a car as it was winter time, but I decided to fly as I was still holding down a job at that time. After I flew in and met up with the other Henchmen, we began to party. We spent many days in a clubhouse doing nothing but drinking and taking dope.

I used to boast to people that I would never get hooked on drugs, that I was the master, and that it would never control me. How wrong I was! I didn't understand the evil effects drugs have on your mind and body. I got so used to taking drugs that I wouldn't even ask what I was eating anymore. Somebody would say, "Open your mouth, Hochie," then throw in a pile of pills. I would swallow them without question. I could have been eating a hand full of rat poison and I wouldn't have known.

At this particular party, there was a bag of bennies (Benzedrine tablets, uppers) being passed around the room between fifteen to twenty bikers. Every time the bag was passed around, each biker popped a bennie into his mouth. I lost count of how many I swallowed. It could have been fifteen, it could have been twenty, or it could have been more. All I know is that I swallowed enough pills that I couldn't sleep for at least two days.

After I flew back home, I went to work and worked a full shift before finally collapsing and passing out in a corner. That evening at the clubhouse, I wandered onto the back porch stoned out of my head.

Looking out across the backyard towards a laneway, I saw something strange. Through the darkness, I saw a row of police cars behind the clubhouse and policemen were standing behind those cars with shotguns draped over the roof, pointed at me.

Completely intoxicated on liquor, beer, and drugs, it seemed like I was living in a dream world. I remember one of the policemen yelling at me, "Walk this way with your hands up!"

I just laughed at him. "Are you crazy?" I yelled back.

I turned and walked back into the clubhouse. They never did come into the house that evening. I'm not sure why they were just parked out back. Maybe they thought it was crazy for them to come into the clubhouse? When morning came, they just packed up and left without raiding the place. A few different times, members were arrested and charged with abduction and rape charges on young girls. I never got myself involved in those things. I never had a problem with dating a girl, so I never saw a need to force any girl into a bad situation. Some of the other members didn't see things that way and oftentimes got themselves into trouble by forcing girls sexually. Some of those members were put into prison for a number of years, spending between three to six years behind bars for one night of what they believed was pleasure.

My brother eventually worked his way up to becoming president. My mother many times would give room and board to fellow members in her house. She always fed them because they had nowhere else to go and some of them had no family. My mom never agreed with the drug abuse and the life of crime, but she still tried to love us and our friends despite the things we were doing. I also had a praying grandmother. Somebody once said, "If you've got a grandmother that's praying, you might as well give up because they'll never shut up." I thank God that my grandmother got to see me become a Christian before she passed away.

I was able to spend some very special times with her before the Lord took her home. Near the end of my grandmother's life, when she became senile, she couldn't remember me, her children, or where she was—or even her own name. Whenever I asked her a question, she just replied, "I don't know." But when I asked her who Jesus was, my grandmother smiled and said, "Oh I know who Jesus is." Even in her years of senility, she never lost touch with her Lord and Saviour. She would start singing, "Jesus loves me, this I know, for the Bible tells me so!" The last time I saw my grandmother, as I walked out of her room in the hospital, she was smiling, radiating the love and presence of God. When I got home ten minutes later, the phone rang and my uncle told me that Grandma had just passed away and gone home to glory.

In the first year when I was riding as a newcomer, I was expected to do whatever the club required of me. One of the members had turned crown witness against the six Henchmen who had been arrested in the shootout on St. Ledger Street. In street lingo, that person was stamped as a rat. It was part of my job to help get this man, even though I had never met him. One night while I was sitting in the clubhouse with some of the guys, a young man broke into the front door of the house, shouting, "They're in the hotel in St. Jacobs and they're putting it on one of your members." We asked who he was talking about.

This man was a friend of one of the members of our club. He had driven in from that village to bring us word that the person we were looking for and some of his goons were roughing up one of our members. I was the only one who had a car that night, so I became the driver. We all grabbed ourselves a piece of weaponry—whether a hammer, chain, or lead pipe—and we got into my car. We drove out to the village, which was fifteen to twenty minutes away. As I was driving, at high speed, I remember thinking to myself, *I really don't want to be doing this. I really don't want to hurt this guy. I don't even know who he is.* Yet because I was a member, I was a slave. I could not free myself from the things I was doing.

When we got to the village, the guy who had come to our clubhouse screamed out, "There they are! Over there!"

A car was parked on the other side of the road. For some reason, this man and his new friends had pulled over while they were vacating the village. That gave me enough time to do a u-turn, pull in front of him, and cut him off so they couldn't get away. I slammed on the brakes and threw the car into park. We all got out of the car at the same time and began to walk towards their vehicle.

There were maybe five guys in the car, three in the front and two in the back. As they saw us coming with our chains, pipes, and hammers, everyone bailed out of the car and began running away, screaming. The only person who couldn't get out of the car in time was the man we were looking for, a fairly big man with large biceps. He seemed like he would be a good scrapper, a man who could fight his way out of anything, yet he had a terrible fear of going to prison. That's why he ratted out the other members and became a crown witness.

Realizing he was outnumbered and we had weapons, he felt that this may be the end of his life.

What am I doing here? I thought to myself. *I don't want to be here. I don't want to be doing this.*

Yet something was driving me to do something I abhorred. The powers of hell are very strong, and demons can push you to do things you never dreamed you would ever do.

I wanted the prestige of being in the club. I wanted the guys to think I was tough. I wanted to belong. But I didn't want to hurt this man.

As we approached the car, one of the members smashed out the headlights. I looked inside and I'll never forget what I saw. This huge hulk of a man was curled up in the fetal position, begging for his life. I thought to myself, *There are no heroes when it comes to dying. There are no heroes when your life is being threatened.* No matter how tough he was when he was in the club, no matter how big his muscles were, he knew his life was in danger. I don't think any one of us that night intended to kill him. I think every one of the guys with me meant only to rough him up and scare him. They definitely wanted him to think they were going to take him out, however, and that could lead to disaster.

In the years that I rode as a Henchman, I knew of only two or three guys who were really capable of murder. The rest only boasted of being that tough. I knew deep inside my heart that these particular men didn't want to take a life.

As we kicked at him and tried to get him to come out of the car, he dove out between me and one of the other members, trying to escape. The member across from me had a lead pipe in his hand and was very angry. He swung the pipe, and he just missed the man's head by an inch.

He swung so hard that the pipe sunk into the back door, literally ripping the metal of the car door open. Had he connected with his head, he would have killed him instantly.

I believe now, as I look back, that God was watching over me. I really feel that the Lord made sure this young man got away so we would not be able to hurt him. I don't know why God chose me, but I'm thankful that He loved me enough to stop this incident. Had it not been for the grace of God, I could be sitting today in a penitentiary for the rest of my life for killing that person. The guy was able to scramble to his feet and run down the street screaming.

It was late at night, so lights came on in the surrounding houses. Someone phoned the police. One of the members said, "Let's get out of here." Rather than chase him down the road, we all went back to the car, got in, and drove away. We threw our weapons out the car window. In case the police pulled us over, they wouldn't find those things in the car.

When we got back to the clubhouse, we sat completely silent, just staring at each other. The man who had ripped open the car door with the lead pipe was shaken. He looked over at me and said, "Hochie, if there's one thing I've found out tonight, I know that I could have killed a man. Had I connected with his head instead of that car door, he would have died."

We just shook our head in agreement. We knew what he was saying was true. He really didn't want to kill, but he could have in a moment of anger. By the grace of God, we were able to escape that night with just our egos torn to pieces.

Chapter 4

BURYING OUR BROTHERS

Not everything that happened while I was in the club was totally bad. There were some good times and special moments with different members and their girlfriends. As a matter of fact, some of the girls who rode on the back of our bikes came from very wealthy and influential homes, some from good upbringings. We even had a couple of members who came from Christian homes with Spirit-filled parents.

At Christmas time, during our annual Henchmen banquet, many of the members dressed up in suits and the girls in nice dresses. There was a hard and fast rule that nobody could get overly drunk or disorderly—and no drugs. There was absolutely no fighting or the sergeant of arms would tend to the problem and expel you from our own banquet. I'm sure other members of the club and their girlfriends were crying out in their hearts to be free. They also wanted to get out of this violent lifestyle filled with alcohol, drugs, and violence. No matter how hard many of us tried, we couldn't break the cycle that held us prisoner.

The problem is that there is pleasure in sin, for a season, but eventually you reap what you sow. *He that sows to the wind shall reap a whirlwind* (Galatians 6:7–8, Hosea 8:7). Some people think that by nature we are good people, but the Bible teaches that we are sinners by nature; we are a fallen race and we need a Saviour. If you don't think that you're a sinner from birth, answer this simple question: why do you have to teach all children how to be good, but you never have to teach them how to be bad? The correct answer is, they know by their sin nature how to be bad. Children know how to lie and steal a cookie. They know how to disobey parents, fight with siblings, and generally misbehave. Parents spend all their time trying to teach them how to be good. The only way to get free from sin is through the shed blood of Jesus Christ. Only faith in Jesus Christ can set the captives free.

The one thing that caused the most depression and battling in my life was the loss of my friends. I attended far too many funerals of young men and women who hadn't yet reached their twenty-fifth birthday. We lost members from our own club, as well as having to attend the funerals of members from other clubs. One such club was The Wild Ones, with whom we were allied. The president hit a car broadside and was killed instantly. After every funeral and burying our brothers, we would go back to the clubhouse to party, drink, and do our drugs. We called it a wake, which was a way of celebrating their lives, yet there was a tremendous sadness inside us that we couldn't overcome. The sadness, I know now, came from living hopeless lives and ending up with hopelessness beyond the grave. There had to be more to life than "eat, drink, and be merry, for tomorrow we die."

The first friend I lost while I was in the club was Frog. One night, he was sitting in one of the hotels drinking a pitcher of beer with his mother. He'd had a little bit too much alcohol flowing through his veins to control the power of his motorcycle, but he got on his bike in downtown Waterloo and screamed up Main Street. He went around a sharp curve and jumped the curb in front of a beer store. As the motorcycle roared across the median and sidewalk, it careened into a tree and killed Frog instantly. His mother, who was walking home from the hotel, was the first to come upon the body of her son. She picked him up in her arms and began to cry, but it was too late and he was already gone. There was nothing anyone could do to bring him back.

Another young man, who we called Dice, asked me if I would sponsor him to join up with the Henchmen. I had already been in the club for two or three years and was extremely depressed. No one knew I was depressed, though, as I would always laugh and smile and party. I didn't want to sponsor him because my own life was falling apart. I was reluctant to drag him into this kind of a life. He kept asking me, and finally I gave in, against my own conscience, and sponsored him to become a member. He began to drink heavy and take drugs just like me and the rest of the members.

One night after leaving a hotel, he got on the back of another member's motorcycle. As they were riding down Victoria Street in Kitchener, they passed in front of Jimmy's Lunch. The driver cracked the throttle open, but Dice wasn't hanging on at that moment. Because he was drunk and stoned, he rolled off the back of the bike and hit the pavement. His brother, who was following too close behind in a car, ran him over and the back tire of the car ended up on his chest. They couldn't get the car started again because it had stalled. Some of the members literally had to pick the car up to pull him out from under the back wheels.

The police and ambulance came and took him to the hospital. They arrested his brother and put him in a jail cell. A couple of hours later, the police came down and pointed their fingers through the bars and told him that his brother was on a marble slab in the hospital and that he had died. They said that he was responsible for his death. He had to lie in that little cell and think about that all night.

One thing I've noticed about life is that there's not a lot of love in the world without Jesus Christ. No matter if you're a gang member or police officer, whether you walk the halls of Parliament or you're a doctor or a nurse, a lawyer or leper of society, love is in short supply. Society thought we were the scum of the earth. Many people would have loved to see us get locked up, with the key thrown away, never to get out of prison again. I don't blame them, because we did a lot of bad things for which we definitely should have been locked up. But people seem to forget that all have sinned and come short of the glory of God. You may be a drug addict in the gutters of society, a prostitute standing on the street corner, or a bike gang member. Or you might come from a good, moral home and a rich family and be a model citizen. Whatever the case, we are all sinners and we need Jesus Christ as our Saviour.

On another night, a member named Popeye met with disaster. He had a bit too much to drink and too many drugs. He hit a hydro poll at high speed on his bike and was killed instantly.

We went to funeral after funeral. Every time a member died, it drove me a little deeper into depression and sadness.

The young man whose death bothered me most was a person we used to call Slick. He was a fun-loving guy, but he was so lost in his life. His father had died of drinking from cirrhosis of the liver. One day, his mother found her husband in the bed motionless. He had gone to sleep drunk and never woke up in the morning.

After the funeral, Slick came home from school with his brother but they couldn't find their mother. Finally, when they went into the basement, they found her hanging from a beam. She had committed suicide and left a note saying that she wasn't able to face life and live alone without her husband and their father. Now Slick and his brother were all alone with no mother, no father, and no place to go for family. Slick's brother moved out west and became a mainliner drug addict. The last I heard was that he died on the streets with a needle broken off in his arm. Nobody knew if it was an overdose, murder, or suicide, but nobody really cared. They just buried him and forgot him.

Slick had no family, so he came to the clubhouse and asked to join our club. He wanted to become a member of the Henchmen so he could have brothers to ride with and have a family. If only a Christian had gotten a hold of him. If only he would have found a family in Christ rather than the Henchmen, he may still be alive today. After becoming a member and getting his crest, his life became increasingly dangerous. He wasn't only a drug abuser, but also a drug dealer. At times he would come into my mother's house with rolls of one hundred dollar bills as fat as your hand. He would throw them at my mom and say, "Here, Ma, hang on to those for me." Then he would laugh. All the gang members called my mother Ma, because she treated them like her own children and gave them a lot of love despite their lifestyle.

Slick used to carry marijuana around, not in little plastic bags but in huge duffle bags. He constantly had cocaine, crack, speed, and different drugs on his person. One night he was in a high-speed chase with the police after a shootout between his van and another car on the expressway in Kitchener. After rolling the van over, the police surrounded him with guns drawn. He could have easily been killed that night. You can only escape death so many times when you're living such a violent lifestyle. On this occasion, he survived.

If money could buy happiness, he had it all. He had a brand new Harley Davidson. He bought himself a Cadillac. He had his own apartment with the best sound equipment money could buy, diamond rings on his fingers, and a girl on each arm. When it came to material things, he had it all, but he had no joy, no peace, and no happiness. There was no purpose to his life.I remember looking into his eyes one day. "Man, Slick," I said, "you're living in the fast lane. If you don't get out, you're going to die young." He just laughed at me and walked away.

Not long after that, he was riding from Guelph to Fergus beside another member of the Henchmen, hopping from hotel to hotel. For some unknown reason, he pulled into the passing lane and cracked open the throttle on his Harley, taking the motorcycle up over a hundred miles per hour. Coming over a hill, he impacted with a car head-on and was killed instantly. Things had finally caught up with him and he just couldn't take it anymore. He had been living on the edge and the enemy pushed him over, taking his life at a very young age.

One time after I was arrested, I thought about my friends who had died so young. I also thought about my own life, which was falling to pieces. I laid my head on my pillow in that jail cell and began to cry. I put my face into the pillow because I didn't want anyone in the cell next to me to hear me cry. The other inmates would have put it on me in the yard the next day. You wouldn't want them to think that a big, tough biker was crying, that he was weak and showed any sign of emotion.

There are many men and women in prisons today all over Canada and America who bury their faces in their pillows every night and cry out for help. Yet there's nobody listening, nobody who seems to care. They feel all alone.

Jesus cares, and He sees every one of them. God said in His Word that if we seek Him with all our heart, we shall find Him (Jeremiah 29:13). God said, *"For I know the thoughts that I think toward you, saith the Lord, thoughts of peace, and not of evil, to give you an expected end"* (Jeremiah 29:11). That night when I cried in my pillow, I prayed, "God, I'm so depressed, so broken, and so lonely. I know I'm just a piece of garbage and I know that You hate me and that You'll never let me into heaven." I knew that if there was a hell, that's where I was going. Yet I asked Him only one little thing: "God if You are out there and if there's any way possible, could you please help me?" That's not a very religious prayer, and I didn't even think God was listening. I prayed it from my heart and I know now that God not only heard my prayer, He began to work in my favour.

I had an experience one night in jail I will never forget. It was kind of like a dream or a vision. Somehow I saw myself in that little cell, crying into my pillow. Then, all of a sudden, I turned over and looked up at the ceiling of the cell. The roof opened up before me and I could see the universe through the roof of the prison. Way out in the universe, a bright light was coming towards the earth. As the light approached, it got brighter and brighter. When it descended into the atmosphere, I saw the form of a Man inside the bright light. That Man came shimmering down to the outer wall of the prison and passed right through the outer wall, even though it was maybe seven or eight feet thick. He came across the courtyard, through the outer bars of our cell block, and right through a second set of bars into our corridor. Then this bright, shimmering Man came over to my cell. I looked up into His face and knew immediately that it was Jesus Christ. I don't remember saying anything. I just lay in my bed and looked at Him in unbelief.

He put His hand through the bars and laid it on my head. He said, "It's okay, Dale. I'm here."

I then went off into a deep sleep.

When I awoke the next morning, a Sunday, the guard yelled, "Chapel up." This meant that the Salvation Army had come in for a church service. A few guys usually went down to chapel, but not very many. That morning, I decided to go down to church. The night before, while wrestling in my cell and feeling like I was going to die, I thought my punishment would be to stay in there forever. I was filled with fear and wanted to go to church to see if maybe God could help me.

I went down to chapel that morning. They sang and preached a little bit and talked to us after the service. When I went back to my corridor, all the guys in my cell block were standing there, waiting for me. I was the only one from our cell block who had gone to church. Some of those guys had done some pretty horrendous things. One young man had taken a shotgun and had committed an armed robbery at a service station the night before. Another one had been in a hotel brawl and broke a beer bottle on the side of a table and jabbed it into a man's face. Needless to say, these were pretty tough guys.

They laughed and taunted me as I walked back into my cell block, saying, "Hey tough guy, the big biker going to church." One of them called out to me, "Hey Henchman! Do you believe in God?"

I looked at the cell and knew I was going to be locked up again that night. I dreaded the thought of denying that I believed in God, and maybe dying in that cell without hope, so I looked at those young men and said, "Yeah, I believe in God."

They began to laugh even harder.

After they quieted down, I looked across the corridor at them and said, "Do you guys believe in God?"

Every one of them stared at me. Then they just turned around and walked away, going back to whatever they had been doing before. Not one of them would deny God, because they were going to be locked up that night, too. They weren't going to let go of that little thread of hope, no matter how much they laughed at me.

When push came to shove, they weren't about to deny that they believed in God. Everyone needs to believe in something! Jesus said that whoever believes in Him shall be saved (Romans 10:9). What hope do any of us have here on earth if there is no life beyond the grave, if there's no hope of a loving God who will redeem us and save us from our sins and give us eternal life with Him?

I never served any long prison terms like some of my friends. I always had good lawyers and was able to beat the charges. It's not that I didn't deserve to go to jail, it was that I always got good breaks and beat my charges on technicalities. I always made sure I had some of the best lawyers in the city.

Sometimes our gang members would go all the way to Toronto to get big city lawyers to fight their rape and assault cases. One time I was up on assault charges from a big fight we'd had with some university students up at the beach on a long weekend. Some of the other guys and I drove up for our court case, which was out of town. Because of drinking and partying the night before, we all got up late and started drinking again before we went to court. We actually arrived an hour late. Stumbling out of the car and going up the steps to that courthouse, the lawyer I had hired came out the front door. He told us to turn around and go back home. He'd already gotten the charges dropped. He knew the judge personally and he'd had a little talk with him in the back room. They worked out an agreement. I don't know what was said or what really happened. All I know is that I was happy to be walking away from that courthouse.

The thing I didn't realize was that I was already in a prison, I just didn't have any bars around me. It was a prison of my own making. It was a supernatural prison, and I was hedged in by demonic powers on every side. I was a captive and I couldn't get free.

Chapter 5

DESCENDING INTO THE DARKNESS

As the darkness continued to close in around my life, I realized that my use of drugs had gotten out of control. I was feeling the rumblings of hell and the thunder of heaven.

Around this time, God began to thunder into my life supernaturally, while the devil tried to destroy me completely. I never considered myself to be a drug addict, as we had a rule in the club that no members were allowed to do needles. People who ended up mainlining on speed or crack could not be trusted; they would sell their own mothers to get the next hit. I did, however, get heavily involved in other chemicals such as THC (tetrahydrocannabinolic) acid, mescaline, marijuana, hash oils, bennies, and other chemicals of which I had no idea what I was eating. I had a couple of major overdoses, and at different times I ended up in the hospital because of ingesting too many drugs for my body to handle. It seemed that every time I went on a bad trip, I saw the demonic realm. It was like Lucifer himself was out to take my life and cast me into a lost eternity at a young age.

Sometimes I wonder if the devil actually knew that God had a call on my life. Maybe he knew that if he didn't take me out young, one day I may end up preaching the gospel for Jesus. You cannot underestimate the satanic realm. I had to deal with powerful demonic forces during my years in the club. Since becoming a Christian, I have continued to deal with evil powers beyond human imagination.

According to Isaiah 14 and Ezekiel 12, Lucifer was God's mightiest angel, the anointed cherub who covers. Next to Jesus Christ, he had the most power of any of God's creation. Revelation tells us that he took one third of God's angels down with him when he was cast out of heaven. That could mean that Satan has literally billions of fallen angels. God called them stars, and we know that the stars of the universe cannot be counted. These fallen spirits are known as demons, working on Satan's behalf. They bring destruction, heartache, and pain to millions of people and families.

I watched young people under demonic influence dig through garbage bags looking for dirty needles. They were so desperate to crank up, looking to get some cocaine back into their veins. These garbage bags seemed so dirty and filthy that even a rat wouldn't go into them. They would find dirty needles, fill them up with drugs, and plunge them into their veins. Then they would end up in the hospital sick from overdoses and infected with hepatitis.

One night, some young men came in from Toronto with a girl who was a heroin addict. They partied with us in an apartment I was renting at the time, and she was coming down cold turkey off of drugs. They had hit her up with some dope when they were in Toronto and she was beginning to get the bends, shakes and the sweats. It's a terrible thing coming down off a high from mainlining. It's a living hell unless you can get those drugs back into your body very quickly. She begged these drug dealers from Toronto to give her another hit, but they just laughed and made fun of her. She was so desperate for drugs that she went into the kitchen, pulled a knife out of the drawer, and began cutting her arm from her wrist to her elbow, trying to kill herself. Blood had spilled all over the kitchen when we finally stopped her and took away the knife. We should have taken her to a hospital; we should have gotten her medical attention. The problem was that it would have brought the police down on us, and nobody wanted the cops coming to investigate. So rather than take her to a hospital, we just bandaged up her arm with old bedsheets, some dirty old thing that should have been thrown into the garbage.

After we wrapped up her arms and stopped the bleeding, one of the drug dealers with a bag of dope said to her, "Look, I'll crank you up with one more hit if you go get me a pack of cigarettes at the store." It was the middle of February, very cold, and snowing on a Sunday afternoon. The nearest store that was open was probably two miles away. She walked in the freezing cold with a bandaged arm to buy a pack of cigarettes. When she got back, they cranked her up for a couple more hours. That's how desperate she was.

That's exactly what demonic powers do to a person who is held by their power. They will drive you beyond anything you could imagine. You become a drug addict with a hopeless addiction.

One night, I overdosed. I don't remember how it happened and I don't even remember where I was. All I remember is that I ended up in the hospital, lying on a bed in the emergency room. I turned my head sideways and looked through the bars of the bed. I looked straight into the face of Lucifer himself. He wasn't really ugly. The Bible tells us that he was a beautiful angel, but I can honestly say he was very evil. Nothing I saw in him was desirable or good. His face and eyes were full of absolute evil. It sent shivers up my spine.

It's going into a supernatural realm. He never talked to me, but I could hear what he was thinking. His thoughts seemed to say, *You belong to me and that I am coming to get you.* Young people don't realize that psychedelic drugs open their spirits to a supernatural realm. It's not all hallucinations and seeing things that aren't really there. Many times you're actually piercing a realm you normally cannot see with the natural mind. It's a supernatural realm of evil, death, and destruction. As a matter of fact, drugs and a life of rebellion opens your spirit to demon possession. I believe that I had demons in my life and that I became demonized, but not totally possessed. The reason I believe this is because after a couple of years of doing drugs, I only had to touch drugs on my tongue to begin to hallucinate. I didn't even have to swallow them. Before the chemical ever got into my bloodstream, I would see bizarre things upon entering a demonic realm, a realm of evil where you really don't want to be. Some young people have descended into that darkness and never returned. They never came back from the last trip. They went too far, one too many times.

I always believed there was a God. I believed there was a heaven and a hell and a devil. I also believed that I was going to hell, not heaven.

Nobody had to tell me I was an evil, wicked person. I knew that from the lifestyle I was living.

I had a very strange experience one night that I could not explain. Now that I'm a born-again Christian, I understand that it was a supernatural battle of good against evil, Jesus Christ against the powers of hell. It was thunder from heaven!

I was riding from Kitchener to New Hamburg one night, hopping from hotel to hotel. I had been drinking heavily and had a lot of drugs in my body. I remember seeing a gigantic devil fill the horizon before me. At the end of the road, a huge red head rose up with horns. This head came over the horizon in the darkness and looked at me with flaming eyes. As this evil face loomed higher and higher in the atmosphere, I felt like I was riding into the mouth of a giant devil. Satan had filled the entire night sky and I was riding straight into the clutches of his evil grip. Because I was stoned, I believed it was just another part of the hallucinations. I tried to shake it off, blinking as I rode my motorcycle down the highway, hoping it would go away.

When we arrived at New Hamburg, we went into the hotel. I felt evil everywhere. I felt demonic power pressing down on my life, trying to destroy me. I remember being very afraid that night, but I dared not show it to my fellow bikers. Fear was a sign of weakness.

There were maybe twenty to twenty-five members in the hotel drinking and partying with a lot of the rounders from that town (guys who just hang out with bikers).

After seeing that huge devil on the horizon, I began to think to myself, *Satan is here. He's inside this hotel and I've got to find him.* I could feel his evil presence. You do some strange things when you're on drugs, drinking heavily. You start thinking abnormally. The thing I didn't realize was that the devil was controlling all of us, that we were all under satanic influence and power. Demonic power is more prevalent when you give demons liberty and power to work in your life.

I began looking around the hotel, trying to locate this evil power. While looking around, I kept thinking, *I know the devil's here and I've got to locate him before he destroys me.*

All of a sudden, I looked to the other end of our table at one of my fellow members, whom we called Diablo. He was a really strange fellow. Sometimes he would growl and vomit up large amounts of phlegm. When I looked at him, his eyes locked onto mine and we stared at each for a while. I felt like I was looking into the eyes of Satan himself.

That's him, I thought. *That's the devil. He's inside one of my friends.*

I never spoke a word and I never said a thing to Diablo. He never spoke to me or said anything to me, either. We just sat there for what seemed like hours, staring at each other, yet it was probably only a few brief seconds—a minute at the most. When you're locked in a supernatural battle and you go into a supernatural realm, things cannot be comprehended by the flesh or the natural mind. I had entered into this supernatural arena before, but always on the demonic side.

I began to speak to this man in my mind. I never used my mouth; I only threw my thoughts towards him. I said, *You are the devil. I know who you are and I command you to leave this place.* I never used the name of Jesus, because I didn't know that you could. I was not a Christian. I had no power or authority in that area. But somehow, something supernatural began to happen. Maybe God honoured the fact that I was becoming more aware of satanic power and wanting to get free. Maybe because Jesus had chosen me to preach the gospel. Maybe He was intervening for me that night in the hotel. I don't know what happened with this man, and I have no idea what he was thinking.

One thing I do know is that the thunder was beginning to sound. I stared at him, and in my mind I commanded him to leave. All of a sudden he stood up and pulled off his Henchmen motorcycle crest. To the amazement of everyone around that table, he threw his patch down and said, "I quit." He then turned and walked out of the hotel.

I will never forget that night or that experience. I believe that the power of God somehow drove him from that place. A few weeks later, he did come back to the clubhouse and rejoin the club, though. I had some very strange encounters with him after that night. There were times when he would growl like an animal.

One time he called me on the phone and asked me a question I could not answer about another member. When I couldn't satisfy him, he growled in unbelievable tones on the other end of the phone. He was thousands of miles away in British Columbia at the time and I was in Ontario. I felt shivers of evil go up my spine knowing that demonic power had so taken hold of this young man; the powers of hell were speaking through him! Those growling noises were inhuman and impossible for him to imitate. They were demonic voices from a demon-possessed man.

The most horrible time I can recall in my life was when I began writing the first chapter of this book on a farm in northern Ontario. We had been up there partying for the weekend with the Coffin Wheelers, who at one time were known as the Plague. This was a pretty rough club in a pretty rough area. They were making their own headlines. I remember partying with them one night in a hotel. There were maybe forty of us. Usually when we went into a hotel and began to make trouble, most people were too afraid to intervene or do anything.

As we laughed, drank, and partied, one of the members found out that the police chief's daughter was in the hotel. Bike gang members and police have never been known to get along very well. When they heard she was in the same hotel, they became angry. One of the members grabbed hold of this woman and bodily threw her out the back door into the alleyway. He told her to get out and never come back. The problem was that these members didn't realize that you can't just throw the daughter of the police chief out the back door without consequences—unless you want the entire police force coming down on you with swift justice. And that is exactly what happened.

Less than half an hour later, the police had surrounded the hotel and were coming in the door by the dozens. They entered the bar and began to apprehend and forcefully subdue us. Two police officers had one of my friends down on the floor and were trying to handcuff him. I ran over and tried to assist him. I took a pitcher of beer and poured it over the policeman's head and told him to cool off and let my friend go. As I was pouring the beer, somebody bashed in the front of my head with a blunt object. I don't know who it was, whether it was a policeman with his billy club or somebody from the hotel; someone was trying to bring down vengeance on my life for making theirs miserable.

Blood ran down between my eyes, and a severe head wound opened up. I didn't fall to the floor, but the whole room went black and I literally saw thousands of stars. People talk about seeing stars when they get hit in the head. That's exactly what happened; stars were coming at me from every direction. Finally, through a hazy blur, I made my way to a doorway to try and get some air so I wouldn't pass out. When I got to the doorway, two policemen who were just entering grabbed me, one on each side, and hauled me back into the hotel, flinging me to the floor. Blood dripped from my head, turning the carpet red. They handcuffed me and eventually began loading us into police cars and patty wagons.

As they dragged me out of the hotel, I remember seeing what looked like hundreds of people lined up on the streets. They came to watch the police drag one biker after another out of the hotel, taking them to prison. Fire trucks and police cruisers were everywhere. They had called the fire department in to hose us down in case any of us tried to get away. Because I had my head split open, my whole face and shirt ran red with blood. As they took me to the police car, a group of teenage girls standing on the sidewalk were horrified. They screamed and put their hands over their eyes, horrified at the way I looked with my head wound.

They threw me into a police cruiser and took me down to the police station with the other members. When they got us into the basement, one of the members was really angry and called one of the police officers "Porky Pig." That was the last thing he should have said, because that brought down more beatings and suffering on the rest of us.

As I said earlier, I have a great respect for policemen now. Most of the police are good, moral, and honourable people. However, while some policemen went by the book, others tended to mete out their own personal frustrations on those they arrested. Even though we deserved everything we got, it still wasn't the right thing for anyone in law enforcement to do. I only pray God would give police officers a compassionate heart for those in their custody. There are Christian policemen I know who even pray for those who are in trouble with the law. Today I stand behind every officer who upholds the laws of our land, and I thank God that they keep our nation safe.

After I gave my life to Christ and became a Christian, I started getting invitations to speak in prisons and high schools. I did a lot of street work, and some church organizations wanted me to come and share my testimony. One time I got a phone call from a police officer. He said that the Waterloo Regional Police wanted me to be the guest speaker at their annual Christmas banquet. About four hundred people, including policemen and their wives, attended. These were the very men who used to arrest me and put me in jail. I now shared with them the love and power of God to change a drug-addicted, alcoholic, demon-possessed biker and make a Christian preacher out of him. Many policemen came up to me after that evening of sharing and told me that their lives had been changed.

Two brothers who I believe were twins came up and told me that they used to get angry at people who were abusive. They said, "From now on, whenever we arrest anybody, we're going to pray for them as we put them in the cruiser. Even though they are good moral people, they still need Jesus as their Saviour." Romans 3:23 says that all have sinned and come short of God's glory. Who would have ever thought that a member of the Henchmen Motorcycle Club, with a notorious reputation all across Canada, would end up speaking at a major police banquet? God works in mysterious ways, His many wonders to perform.

A couple police officers hauled me into a separate room after I told one the officers that I needed to have my head stitched. I was still bleeding badly. After they took me into the other room, two cops holding onto me, a detective came in and looked in my direction. As he walked across the room, I saw anger in his face. He took his foot and drove it up between my legs, giving me a severe kick to my groin.

After that blow, the officers dragged me out into the alleyway behind the station. Two other officers were waiting out by a cruiser; it was the four of them, and just me alone. Two of the policemen grabbed my hair, one on each side, and drove my face into the roof of the cruiser. They battered my injured head on top of the cruiser, trying to make me suffer even more. With that, they put me into the back of the police cruiser, with a cop on each side and two in the front. As they drove away, I remember thinking to myself, *They're going to take me out into the country. They're going to put a bullet in my head, and then tell people that I tried to escape.*

The officer in the passenger seat had a billy club, and he was patting it into the palm of his other hand. He was just waiting for me to say something so he could hit me again.

"We're taking you to the hospital," said one of the officers beside me. "If you say one thing before we get you there, you're in trouble."

I might have thought I was tough, but I definitely wasn't stupid. I wasn't going to open my mouth just so they could beat my head in even more.

I sensed heaviness in my chest and it felt like I couldn't breathe. I opened my mouth and took a deep breath, trying to relieve the pressure I felt. When I took this deep breath, one of the policemen said, "We warned you."

Even though I hadn't said a word to them, they were looking for any excuse to beat me again. With that, the two policeman began to pound and punch on my body. I don't believe they stopped until we got to the hospital. I became a punching bag until we arrived at the emergency entrance. I was never so glad to see a hospital in all my life.

They dragged me into the hospital and took me into one of the rooms so the doctor could stitch up my head. I didn't get a lot of sympathy from any of the doctors or nurses either, as they'd probably already heard what had happened downtown at the hotel. The doctor looked me over and shaved the hair from the front of my head. He gave me a little bit of a painkiller and then began to stitch my injury. After he finished putting in the stitches, he released me back into the custody of the police.

They were going to take me back to jail, but thankfully the beatings were finished—perhaps because of what happened next. When God thunders from heaven, He does so to get our attention. He uses even the bad things in life to bring glory to His name and salvation to our lost souls. After all, the Bible says in 2 Peter 3:9 that He is *"not willing that any should perish."*

I got out of the emergency ward, the police cruiser had gone back to the city jail. The officers with me had to call for him to return. I sat in the foyer, handcuffed to one of the officers. My face, shirt, and pants were covered in blood. When I looked over at the police officer, I noticed that he had blood splatters on his shirt from hitting me.

"What are you charging me with?" I asked. "Why am I here?"

"Because you beat me up, I've charged you with police assault."

"You're a liar. I never touched you."

He just snickered at me.

After that, a man in a suit came walking by with a briefcase in his hand. He looked like a doctor or lawyer or somebody very important. He saw the policeman all splattered with blood and said to him, "What happened to you?"

The policeman just turned his head away. The man then looked at me and saw that my head was split open and my shirt was full of blood.

"What happened to you?" he asked me.

At that moment, I felt like saying, "This jerk next to me beat my head in." I wanted to tell him what they had done to me in the cruiser. For some reason, I didn't. I just looked at the man and said, "I walked into a door."

With that, the man turned and walked away. He knew I was lying, but I didn't feel that it would do any good to tell the truth. The truth would only get my head beat in again. Maybe because I didn't point my finger at the policeman, he became more lenient with me.

The police didn't touch me again that night. They simply took me back to the station, put me in a cell, and locked me in for the evening.

The next morning we got bail and were charged with various crimes. I myself still had to face a charge of police assault.

When we were released, we found out that they had taken our vests with our club crests and cut them up into little pieces. They were trying to make our life just a little more miserable, and they knew how much we as club members valued our club colours.

I wasn't looking forward to going back to the city to face those charges. Even the mayor was getting in on the situation. The headlines in the paper the next day screamed for justice against these evil bikers, of which I was one. The mayor said that he and the police chief would personally see to it that these clubs were done away with permanently.

They would lock us up and throw away the key and we would never see the light of day again.

The whole city was in an uproar. Everybody seemed to be angry. I thought to myself, *This is going to be a tough one to get out of. I'm probably going to end up going to jail for a long time.*

I must make a note here that I became a Christian before I had to go back and answer those charges. I asked God for mercy, that I wouldn't get any jail time, as I wanted to be free to share the gospel on the streets. However, I didn't try to make any deals with God. I simply said that if I did go to jail, I would still be a Christian on the inside and share Jesus with other inmates. When I finally went to court, the crown attorney told the judge that they'd lost my file so they were dropping the charges. Praise the Lord!

Not long after, I was back at the clubhouse a few miles outside the city. We were drinking and doing drugs, living our usual wild and insane life. That particular night, I did more drugs than I had ever done in my entire life. I was drinking electric wine and somebody came along with a bag full of dope. I started popping pills and blotters out of that bag. I was so drunk and stoned that I had no idea what I was eating. It could have been rat poison and I would have eaten whatever they gave to me. This night, as the thunder of heaven began to roll, my life turned in a dramatic new direction.

Any time there was free dope going around the circle or somebody had something for me to swallow, all they had to do was say, "Open your mouth," and they could throw in whatever they desired. With the electric wine, the straight liquor, the beer, and the bag full of dope, I had enough chemicals in my body to kill an elephant. I don't know why I'm alive today; I don't know why I'm here. I almost died on a couple of occasions. It is only the grace of God that I didn't die. He saw that one day I would yield my life to Him and preach the gospel for His glory. At that time, He was the furthest thing from my mind. Not only did I not ever want to be a preacher, I never dreamed that God would ever want me to preach. But Jesus did say in the Bible, *"Go out into the highways and hedges, and compel them to come in, that my house may be filled"* (Luke 14:23). That's where I lived, in the gutters of society, and Jesus came and rescued me.

Satan and demons had come to destroy me and take me to hell, but God intervened. I believe it was because I had a praying grandmother. While standing on the front porch of that clubhouse that night, I entered a satanic realm that I almost never returned from. I took a swallow from the bottle of beer I was holding; when I put it down, I looked out into the dark field. It was sometime around midnight and very dark and foggy. All of a sudden, the field exploded into flames.

I looked around at the motorcycles out in front of the clubhouse, and they all exploded into flames, too. I dropped my beer, spun around, and looked at the clubhouse behind me. It, too, exploded into flames. Everything was on fire around me. I looked around the front yard and saw what only a few minutes before had been my friends, my fellow bikers and their girlfriends, partying, laughing, and drinking. I still saw the bodies, but I no longer saw their faces. I saw demons laughing at me, devils on every side trying to torment me. The tire on my motorcycle turned into a serpent and began to hiss.

As I said earlier, people think that when you take hallucinogenic drugs you're only seeing things in your mind, but in reality you're facing a satanic supernatural realm. Drugs open a demonic gate to the soul in order to destroy you and take you to hell. I was full of fear and terror at what I was seeing and feeling. It was as if I was in an eternal, hopeless void with no way of escape. I cried out in front of thirty or forty of my fellow bikers and their girlfriends, "God, if I'm in hell then this is where I belong." I thought I had died and that I had slipped into a lost eternity, an eternal torment. I knew I deserved to be in that place.

The drug overdose took me to the very edge of hell. I could feel the torment of the lost, the weeping and wailing and gnashing of teeth God warned us of in the Bible. I was being supernaturally transported to this horrible place.

My friends heard me cry out to God. They knew I was stoned and having a rough time. They had seen others flip out on dope and were in no mood or condition to help me. They laughed as they came over and grabbed hold of me. They pulled me off the porch and took me out to the field. They stopped by a telephone pole and said to me, "Hochie, this can be your God. You stay here and worship this for the rest of the night." They walked away, laughing. To them this was not cruel or unusual punishment; they were stoned, too, and didn't want to get on a bad trip. When someone started freaking out, we would usually just lock them up in a room until they came down—get rid of them and get them out of our presence so they don't mess up the party and ruin the night.

Unfortunately, some people on drugs never came back. They went on a one-way and never returned. They should have taken me to a hospital. The problem is that people in that lifestyle don't have a lot of love, compassion, and concern for each other. We were supposed to be tough and just suck it up and ride it out ourselves.

I stood there, looking up at that telephone pole and thinking to myself, *This is not God. I've got to get out of here.*

I ran out into the field. Standing out there by myself, I felt the horrors of a lost eternity press in on me—the outer darkness, the eternal torment, the flames of God's judgment, the thirst that is never quenched. I felt everything the Bible warns us of if you die without Christ. I didn't know how to escape the judgment of hell, so it seemed hopeless. I didn't know that Jesus came to die in our place and take our punishment. No one ever told me that all you had to do was call on His name and believe on Him for salvation. God's Word tells us:

> *For whosoever shall call upon the name of the Lord shall be saved.* (Romans 10:13)

> *For the wages of sin is death; but the gift of God is eternal life through Jesus Christ our Lord.* (Romans 6:23)

The problem is, I never knew these things because I had never heard that great message of love and forgiveness.

I can't take this, I thought. *I can't handle it. I've got to kill myself. I've got to die.*

I had thoughts of suicide. I thought that if I could just find a rope and put it over the limb of the tree, I could end this.

There, in the middle of that field, I heard a voice: "How can you kill yourself if you're already dead?"

I stopped to think about that for a moment. *Yes, I'm in hell. I've died already. I can't kill myself. If you're dead you can't die.*

Nothing was making sense to me.

Then I heard the voice again: "Maybe you're not dead."

Now I was really confused. I was feeling all this torment and seeing all these demonic things, and then I was having a conversation with myself.

"Maybe there's a God out there who loves you," the voice said. "Maybe there's hope."

When I heard that word—hope—it hit me like a freight train. *Maybe there's a God out there who loves me and cares for me. Perhaps I'm not dead.*

I then eliminated the thought of suicide.

Everyone needs hope, and that voice gave me hope again. In hell there is no hope. You are separated from your creator for all eternity if you die without receiving God's gift of salvation through Christ. I had cried out to God on the front porch of that clubhouse, and I asked God to help me. I called out to a God I didn't know, who I believed hated me and wanted to destroy me. It is not God who wants to destroy us; it is the devil who is the destroyer of lives. God knew me, He knows you, and He knows your heart.

And ye shall seek me, and find me, when ye shall search for me with all your heart. (Jeremiah 29:13)

I had been praying in jail cells and in my own bed at night, trying to find God, but I had thought He didn't care or wasn't listening. If we really want to find Him, He will reveal Himself to us. Now, as a Christian, I know that I did hear a loving God speak to me that night when I was dying on a drug overdose. Parents, please don't stop praying for your children, no matter how far they fall. One day your prodigal will come home.

After hearing that voice, I decided to go back to the clubhouse and phone my mother, who was three hundred miles away in another city. I knew that if my mother was alive, I would know for sure that I wasn't dead; I would know I wasn't in hell. I felt if anybody was going to heaven, my mother was going to heaven. She was a good woman who treated everyone the same. She even showed love when the police were raiding her house and ripping apart her cupboards looking for drugs and stolen goods (they never found any, because Mom never allowed it in the house). My mom would offer the police a cup of coffee. She just loved everybody. She wasn't a Christian, but she was definitely a loving woman. Some people will sift through a bushel of wheat to find a speck of dirt; my mother would sift through a bushel of dirt to find a speck of wheat. She would only look at the good in your life. She would never look at the bad. She never agreed with our lifestyle, but she also never turned anyone away when they needed her.

Love is a powerful thing. I went back to the clubhouse, picked up the telephone, and made a call to my mom.

She picked up the phone, not knowing what was happening to me in the middle of that dark night. When she answered, I said, "Mom is that you?"

"Yes, Dale. What's wrong?"

"Mom, is that really you?"

"Yes,"

I cried out, "Mom, Mom! Don't hang up. If you do, one of us is going to die."

With that, I ripped the phone off the wall and broke the connection, leaving her three hundred miles away with a dead line.

My brother and I literally put my mother through hell. She never knew if we were dead or alive. She would get calls in the middle of the night saying that one of her sons had had his head beaten in or was in jail. Now she got a call saying that she was going to die or I was going to die, and then left with a dead line, not knowing what was to happen with her son.

I had thought it was a demon lying to me and impersonating my mother. That's why I ripped the phone off the wall and broke the connection. I ran outside, kicked my Harley over in the dirt, took off my patch, and threw it on the ground. I had a beautiful full dressed Harley Davidson with a custom paintjob, but when you're overdosing, nothing in this life matters. Motorcycles, cars, girls, or parties, nothing is important.

I just wanted the torment to end. I didn't care about anything. It may be hard for some people to understand, but I was fighting for my life in a satanic realm that the natural man cannot comprehend.

I left the clubhouse and walked out to the highway. At first when I got out to the road, I just crossed over to the other side. There was a farmhouse on that side of the road and I banged on the door, completely out of my mind on drugs. A young girl who I think was babysitting some young children came to the door and saw me. She opened the door and let me in to sit down. I think back about that many times. How dangerous it was for her to open that door and let this gang member into her house. But somehow she didn't seem to be afraid of me.

She asked me what was wrong and what she could do to help. She seemed like an angel sent from God. The Bible says that some men entertain angels unaware. I just looked at her in disbelief, wondering why she would even care. Then the thought came to me that she was just deceiving me and was part of a satanic conspiracy to destroy me. I turned and ran out of that farmhouse. She called for me to come back, but I kept running.

I was afraid, lost, and didn't know who I was or where I was going. I felt that I couldn't trust anyone. I ran back out onto the highway. I got to the centre of the road and stood on the white centre line. I saw that line go in both directions into that horrible darkness.

I've got to walk in outer darkness for all eternity, I thought. I just couldn't decide whether to go right or left. A tractor trailer could have run me over and I would have been killed instantly. I know I was literally dying that night. I know that I was on the edge of a lost eternity, yet God still had His eye on me. God has His eye on the sparrow and not one of them will fall to the ground without Him seeing it fall. He knows the very hairs on our head. I know now that it was by God's loving grace that I'm still alive today.

The first car to come along was a police cruiser. I don't believe that was a coincidence, but a divine appointment, an angel sent from God to help me. He swerved around me when he saw me standing in the middle of the road. He stopped his cruiser, put on the lights, got out of his car, and walked back to where I was standing.

"What are you doing in the middle of the road?" he asked.

I looked up at him. "I don't know. What are you doing in the middle of the road?"

He told me to get in the cruiser. I knew how to do that, as I had lots of practice.

We both got into the cruiser. He let me sit in the front seat next to him, which was unusual; police always put us in the back for their own safety.

He had seen the party going on at the clubhouse. "Did you come out of that party?" he asked.

"Yes."

"Who are you? What's your name?"

He didn't speak in a rough or harsh way. He spoke to me as if he cared and was really concerned. I recall looking at his face, and it was shiny, like an angel's face would shine. Stephen's face shone like an angel in Acts 6:15, just before he was stoned to death for preaching the gospel. In hindsight, I believe that this policeman was a Christian. I felt as if I was in the presence of someone who loved me, even though he didn't know me. It had to be the power of the Holy Spirit shining through his life. I haven't seen him or spoken to him since that night, but I believe I will meet him again one day in heaven.

What is this policeman doing in hell? I asked myself. *Henchmen belong in hell. Police go to heaven because they are good people.*

I thought only good people went to heaven. We bikers were the evil people who went to hell. Nothing was making sense to me. I even thought that maybe God had policemen patrolling hell to torment us for the rest of our eternity. I was really messed up! I know now that we are all sinners, and everyone needs a saviour. His name is Jesus!

I took my wallet out of my pocket after he asked me my name. I opened it up and pulled everything out. I threw my money, credit cards, and papers all over the inside of the cruiser. There was paper on the dashboard, on the backseat, and all over the car. Some even landed on top of him.

"There," I said. "If you can find a name, that's who I am. I don't know my name."

This policeman knew I was having a rough time on drugs. He picked up the radio and called for an ambulance.

The ambulance came out from the hospital and they put me in the back with an attendant. As they were driving to the emergency room, something supernatural began to happen. I had never experienced anything like it before. I felt a supernatural power around the outside of that ambulance. I couldn't understand what was happening. I just knew there was power around me.

All of a sudden, this power began to pour into the ambulance. It felt like it was coming through the roof and the windows; it then began to move through my body in wave after wave after wave. As this power passed through my body, I convulsed and shook. I felt like the ambulance had lifted off the road, like a jet taking off. It seemed like I was streaking through outer space at a million miles an hour, like my body was sucked up out of a horrible pit.

Since becoming a Christian, the Lord has given me a scripture to be my testimony:

> *I waited patiently for the Lord; and he inclined unto me, and heard my cry.*
>
> *He brought me up also out of an horrible pit, out of the miry clay, and set my feet upon a rock, and established my goings.*
>
> *And he hath put a new song in my mouth, even praise unto our God: many shall see it, and fear, and shall trust in the Lord.* (Psalm 40:1–3)

As my body was shaking, I hung onto sides of the bed and began to scream out loud, "I'm coming up! I'm coming up!"

I think the ambulance attendant sitting next to me felt like jumping out the back door. I'm sure I scared the life out of him. He probably thought I was completely losing my mind and having a mental breakdown. Something supernatural was happening to me and he had no understanding of it.

All of a sudden the power stopped and I felt myself come back to reality. I looked around and realized that I was lying in the back of an ambulance and that my name was Dale Hoch. I knew who I was and where I was. I wasn't hallucinating anymore. I wasn't seeing demons and devils, blood and fire and horrible things. I realize now that the power of the Holy Spirit had filled that ambulance. God delivered me from those drugs before I even got to the hospital. He literally pulled me back from the edge of a lost eternity. I had enough drugs in my body that I should have been stoned for at least two days, yet in a matter of seconds God cleaned those drugs out of my body supernaturally.

When I got to the hospital and got out of the ambulance, I walked in without being under any drug influence. They pumped me full of downers and I staggered out of the hospital. I felt like I came out more stoned than when I entered.

It was the same power of the Holy Spirit that fell on the believers on the day of Pentecost in Acts 2. It was the same Holy Spirit that healed the sick and raised the dead. It was the precious Comforter that Jesus promised in John 14:26 to send in His name to all those who would believe.

I was not a believer, but I had a grandmother praying for me. I also had a mother who loved me, and I'm sure she was praying also, even though she wasn't a Christian. I found out afterward that some of the Christians back in Kitchener-Waterloo had been praying for me even though their own sons and daughters had been held captive by the devil in our club. They not only prayed for their children, but also for me and for the rest of the members. My deliverance that night was the result of their prayers and also a result of me calling out to God on the front porch of that clubhouse.

When I got out of the hospital, I went to a phone booth and called the other members and told them to come and get me at the hospital. A carload of them came into town to pick me up and take me back to the farmhouse. I began drinking and doing drugs that very next day.

You might think to yourself, *How foolish and how stupid. Why would you ever go back to the alcohol and drugs when you almost died?* I can't explain it. All I know is that God said in the Bible that we are slaves to sin and we cannot free ourselves. We need somebody greater than ourselves to set us free. Jesus Christ said, *"If the Son therefore shall make you free, ye shall be free indeed"* (John 8:36). Jesus also said, *"I am the way, the truth, and the life: no man cometh unto the Father, but by me"* (John 14:6).

I needed Jesus Christ to set me free, but I didn't know how to get there. I didn't know the way of salvation. No one had told me about accepting Christ as my personal Saviour. So I did what I always did: party, drink, do dope, and get arrested.

Dale as a young teenager

Dale & Edith in younger years

Dale in his Henchmen M.C. years

Dale on a Club Run

My mother known to the club members as Ma

Dale & Edith touring on their Harley

Mac & Wife Phyllis with Dale & Edith on holidays

Dale rides with the Chariots of Light Christian Bikers' Club

Pastor Dale and Edith founders of World Outreach Ministries

Dale on his television broadcast Faith On Fire

Chapter 6

THE ROAD HOME

Through all the battles I was going through, God still had His hand on me. As the Lord continued to thunder from heaven, it set me on the road home. Jesus Christ said, *"Ye have not chosen Me, but I have chosen you"* (John 15:16). Ephesians 1:4 says that He *"hath chosen us in him before the foundation of the world."* God doesn't make us be good or bad or cause us to accept or reject Him. We are free will agents and choose whether or not to believe in God. The Bible says that He is *"not willing that any should perish"* (2 Peter 3:9). Because God is all-knowing (omniscient), He knows those who will accept or reject Him long before they ever make that decision. Jesus also said, *"Of them which thou gavest me have I lost none"* (John 18:9). I believe in my heart that anyone on this planet who God knows will surrender to Him; they will find their way home to Jesus Christ and to eternal life.

I still didn't have any idea how to find my way to God or make it to heaven. I didn't know the message of salvation because nobody ever told me how to give my life to Jesus Christ. I had done a lot of praying in my prison cell and on my bed at home at night, but I never really believed that God was listening to me. I did have some encounters with Christians that I believe were divine appointments, so I could begin my journey home to God.

Everyone has divine appointments in their lives: supernatural encounters, people meeting us on the road of life at an appointed time to bring us to an appointed place. I recall one night at the clubhouse when I was stoned on some THC and mescaline. I was almost completely out of my mind on dope and in a daze. While walking around outside, I noticed that someone had come by earlier and dropped a booklet on the front lawn. It surely must have been a born-again Christian directed by the Holy Spirit. When I looked down, I noticed the word "bewitched" written on the cover. I picked it up and began to read this little booklet.

It was the story of a girl who was strung out on drugs, and it was written in comic book form. As I began to read, I thought to myself, *That's me. I'm the one who's stoned on drugs. My friends and I, we're all stoned on drugs.*

I read about how this girl felt hopeless and helpless, and how she was rebelling and running away from her family.

That's me, too. I'm running. I'm on the run.

As I read the booklet, I learned about how she had a praying grandmother. Her grandmother would not quit praying for her.

I have a grandmother who's praying for me. This is my life story.

The girl ended up in the hospital dying of a drug overdose.

This can't be real. This is my booklet. This is my life story. I was in the hospital, I was dying on a drug overdose.

Her grandmother kept praying for her and then she went to the hospital and told her how to receive Christ as her Saviour. In the end, the girl gave her life to Christ and she was forgiven for her sins. She did die, but it showed her going to heaven and being forgiven and living with Jesus for all eternity.

When I finished reading the book, I thought to myself, *Is it possible that God would take drug addicts to heaven? Maybe He would take a biker like me to heaven if only I could find Him.*

I took the book and went out behind the clubhouse. There, a member we called Hammer was digging a hole about six feet long and four feet wide. He was drunk and stoned and had dug the hole down maybe a foot or two. He was standing in this hole and digging away.

"Hammer, what are you doing?" I asked.

He looked up at me. "I'm digging a grave."

"Why are you doing that?"

"Because when I'm finished, I'm going to lie down in this grave and blow my brains out."

He was stoned and really didn't know what he was doing or saying.

Another night, a member who was stoned on drugs was running back and forth through a field, dodging and jumping up and down in the grass. Other members, who were also stoned, watched him run back and forth all night. In the morning, they asked him what he was doing. He simply said that a spaceship had been trying to beam him up; he'd been trying to escape and get away from it.

Another member who was eating dinner, again stoned on drugs, said that the rice got up on the dinner plate and began to dance around on the table.

One thing you don't want to do is get your life messed up on drugs.

"Hammer, you don't need to do that," I said. "Read this little book and it will tell you about heaven and about God."

"Get that garbage away from me," he said with hostility in his voice. "I don't want to see that stuff."

I shook my head and thought to myself. *Yeah. What am I thinking? What am I talking about? I'm a bike gang member. I'm a Henchman. I shouldn't be talking about this stuff.*

Yet I never forgot that little book, and I never forgot the message I read that night. I had been hit by a bolt of God's supernatural lightning.

A little while later, we were up at Crystal Beach partying for the weekend. When there's a bunch of bike gang members together for a few days partying, things can get pretty rough. Not only do you look tough and ragged, but you feel tough and ragged. Most of the members were pretty clean, but one man who rode with us kind of took delight in being as dirty as he could get. He didn't wash for weeks at a time. His pants would literally shine from the dirt on them. When he would ride in the rain, there would be streaks on his neck and face where the dirt washed off.

Very late one night, a couple of members and I were walking down the street laughing, swearing, yelling, and looking for trouble. One of the men was named Grizzly, because he was all hairy with a big woolly head of hair, a big beard, and hair on his chest, legs, and arms. Usually when three or four drunken bike gang members walk down a street late at night, nobody gets in their way. They either did some quick window-shopping as we went by or they crossed to the other side of the street.

This particular night, two young people on the other side of the road came running across and stopped right in front of us. It was a boy and girl, and they looked like they were teenagers. They had big smiles on their faces and they were holding a pile of papers under one arm and a Bible under the other.

"Hey guys," the boy said. "We're having a gospel sing in that field over there tomorrow night. We're going to be singing and preaching about Jesus, and we want you guys to come along."

They just stood there, smiling at us as we stared at them in disbelief.

Normally you would grab them by the collar, punch them in the face, bloody their nose, and push them in the gutter. Kick them and tell them to get lost, you little goof! But this time we couldn't touch them, we couldn't talk, we couldn't do anything. We just stood there, looking at them. I know now that it was because there was more power in them than in us. Two of them and four of us, and we were outnumbered. They weren't afraid of us. We were just lost sinners who needed help. God must have sent angels to hold down our hands and feet, like when Daniel was in the lions' den. God sent His angels to shut the mouths of the lions. As a matter of fact, we couldn't even swear at these kids. God sent an angel to shut our mouths, too!

Finally, the young man said; "Well, are you coming or aren't you?"

"Well, we'll think about it," one of the bigger members said.

And off they went down the street looking for someone else to invite to their gospel meeting. I never forgot the glow on those two young people's faces.

I saw that same glow on the face of the policeman who put me in his cruiser on that dark highway. Because these teenagers were born-again Christians, the glow I saw on their faces was the shine and anointing of the Holy Spirit. Those young people weren't afraid of us because they had the power of the Holy Spirit in their lives, and they were showing the love of Jesus Christ. 1 John 4:18 says that *perfect love casteth out fear: because fear hath torment.*

A couple of years later, after I became a Christian, I was sharing my testimony on a Christian television show called *100 Huntley Street*. I shared the story of those two young people at Crystal Beach. Well, those teenagers just happened to be watching that day. They phoned into the program and said, "We were the two young people who met you on the street that night. We remember you and we remember talking with you."

Isn't it wonderful how God works? By watching a television program, a Christian broadcast, they were able to see the fruit for their labours. All of these encounters with Christians were God's way of directing me to the cross of Calvary. He was slowly and lovingly bringing me to a place where I would finally receive Him as my Saviour. You see, the Lord cannot work in your life before you're ready to receive. God will deal with you and He will send people and circumstances into your life to try to turn your heart towards Him. When the time is right, God will bring you into contact with the truth, when He knows you will be ready to receive. Jesus said, *"Except a man be born again, he cannot enter the kingdom of God"* (John 3:3). I was on a road to rebirth and God was the one guiding me there by thunder and lightning.

Another time, something happened that I find kind of humorous. After a weekend party, we were all pretty burned out. It was a hot Sunday afternoon and we had ridden into a town by the name of Hespeler, about half an hour outside of our city. We had all the motorcycles lined up down the street and we were lying on the sidewalk, nursing our hangovers.

Just across the road from where we were lying down, we saw a couple of people from the Salvation Army dressed in their uniforms. They walked up the sidewalk on the other side of the street with some instruments—a drum, a tuba, a bugle, and a tambourine. They set up their instruments and began to sing old time gospel songs like "Amazing Grace" and "The Old Rugged Cross." They were playing their gospel hymns and sharing from the Word of God.

"I'll take care of these people," I said to the others on the sidewalk. I got up and went over to my motorcycle; I had very loud pipes on my bike at the time. I got on my bike, started it up, and began to rev the engine, trying to drown them out. I figured if I revved my bike long enough, they would get fed up and leave. I revved my motorcycle time and time again: vroom, vroom, vroom. But the louder I revved that motorcycle, the louder they sang. They actually outsang me and I couldn't be bothered to rev the bike anymore. I finally shut it off and went back to sit down with my friends.

When you're serving God with all your heart, mind, and soul, there's a persistence in your life. You won't quit, especially when it comes to a lost soul.

When they finished singing their songs and sharing from the Bible, they finally picked up their instruments and moved on. I made fun of these encounters, but they always made an impression on me. Those people were there on a divine appointment from God. He was still thundering from heaven.

God was beginning to deal with me, and things happened that I now see as the sovereign direction of the Lord to bring me to Himself.

One night in my bedroom, I was feeling really depressed. I picked up a little Gideon Bible that I had gotten in school when I was a young boy. I hadn't opened it in years. I took that tiny Bible and opened it, thinking maybe I could find some hope and help. When I opened it, my eyes fell to a scripture that in human understanding doesn't make any sense at all. You would think when a person is depressed, broken, addicted to drugs, and suicidal, they would read a scripture about love and forgiveness and God's tender care. But that's not what I read. The scripture I read was far different. It talked about the broad road and the wide gate to hell, and that many people passed through the gate. It talked about the straight road and the narrow gate to heaven, and said that few ever find it (Matthew 7:13–14).

I slammed the book shut and thought, *If only a few people are going to find their way to heaven, I'll never get there. I'm lost for sure.*

It only depressed me more. In fact, it really broke my heart. That's why my story is called thunder from heaven, because God had to break me before He could save me. God knew that I didn't need a love message at that time; I needed to be broken so that I wouldn't be destroyed. Jude 22–23 says that some people are saved by compassion (the love message) but that other people are saved by fear pulling them out of the fire (the hellfire and brimstone message). I needed the hellfire and brimstone message because I was hard, indifferent, and cold to the things of God. The love message just wasn't working on me, but I feared God's judgment and justice.

Even God's warning of eternal judgment will bring us to His tender love and forgiveness.

The Bible says that the goodness of God leads us to repentance (Romans 2:4). Even though I was reading about His judgement, it was His goodness leading me! The earlier scripture from Matthew 7 helped bring me under the love and forgiveness of the Lord Jesus Christ. I have since come to understand that the straight road and the narrow gate are not our good religious works. That straight road is red, and it was paved with the blood of Jesus when He died on the cross. The narrow gate is Jesus Himself, as the Bible says: *"for there is none other name under heaven given among men, whereby we must be saved"* (Acts 4:12).

It is the only road to heaven, and that's why it is so straight and narrow. The only thing that can keep you on that road is faith in the Lord Jesus Christ. You must believe your way home to heaven. I lived foolishly, yet God had a verse for me:

> *And an highway shall be there, and a way, and it shall be called The way of holiness; the unclean shall not pass over it; but it shall be for those: the wayfaring men, though fools, shall not err therein.* (Isaiah 35:8)

I came under such deep conviction that I knew I had to end my life in the club before it ended my life on earth. The day I left the Henchmen, I walked into the clubhouse during a club meeting. It was a Sunday afternoon and there were twenty to twenty-five members sitting around having a meeting. I took my patch off and threw it into the middle of the circle.

"I'm quitting," I said. "I'm leaving the club."

If you were a member in bad standing, you would get a pretty rough time whether you wanted to leave or stay. But I was a member in good standing. My whole family was involved in the bike club and my brother was president. Because most of the members really liked me, they never gave me a rough time. They just said, "Hochie, why are you leaving? What's up? What's wrong? What's coming down?"

"I can't tell you," I said. "I can't talk about it. I just have to leave."

I walked out of the clubhouse that day and went down West Avenue in the middle of Kitchener. I felt so lonely and lost. I felt like I didn't have a friend on the planet. Tears ran down my cheeks. I looked up to heaven and said, "God, I'm so lonely, I'm so empty, I'm so hurt. Can You help me, God? Are You there? Do You love me? I need help."

Unbeknownst to me, this was just one more leg on the road home. This was God's leading in my life to bring me to a place where He could save me from my sin. I could leave the gang, I could stop hanging out with my friends, I could try and do all the right things, but that still wouldn't get me into heaven. There is only one way for us to find God. There is only one way to heaven, and that way is faith in Jesus Christ.

One of the most difficult things for me when I came to know Jesus as my Saviour was leaving my family behind. When I walked out of the clubhouse that day, I felt like I had forsaken them. I felt as if I was a traitor to my own family, because I had helped get them into the mess I was leaving. Jesus said, *"If any man come to me, and hate not his father, and mother, and wife, and children, and brethren, and sisters, yea, and his own life also, he cannot be my disciple"* (Luke 14:26). Jesus must be number one, or we cannot be His disciples. It was my willingness to leave my family behind that eventually had a big part in bringing them to Christ. You see, when you put Jesus first, God will honour that and begin to work with your family.

I didn't make any deals with God. After I became a Christian, I even said to Him, "God, if my family never comes to You, I will serve You anyway." It wasn't because I didn't love them; it was because I did love them and I had to put them in God's hand. You see, God is our true Father and our Creator, and Jesus Christ makes us part of the true family of God. I couldn't live in both worlds, so I had to make a choice about who I would serve. They were still caught up in the motorcycle gang and I was on my way to a city *whose builder and maker is God"* (Hebrews 11:10).

I witnessed to my brother so often after becoming a Christian that he got mad enough to punch me out. He actually made a fist and told me to leave him alone.

"If I want to go to hell, I'll go to hell."

God spoke to me that day and said, "Leave him alone. You've told him the way and I will do the rest."

They all eventually came to know Jesus as their Saviour.

Chapter 7

A SUPERNATURAL ENCOUNTER

As my life continued to plummet in a downward spiral, I prayed and asked God for help. But I was continually plagued with doubt and fear, not thinking God cared or would listen to me, a wicked sinner. I just couldn't believe there was any way out of my mess. How was it possible to undo all the wrong of the past years by trying to be good in the future? God knew I desperately wanted to find Him, that I wanted to find a way out, and He was preparing the way. The Bible says, *"And ye shall seek me, and find me, when ye shall search for me with all your heart"* (Jeremiah 29:13).

One Sunday afternoon, I was sitting in a Tim Horton's coffee shop with a few friends. These weren't members of the gang; they were just people who hung out in the same hotels. I used to drink, party, and dance with some of these girls. I tried to warm up to one of them, as I liked her. She didn't want much to do with me, because I was a member of the Henchmen. It didn't help that her cousin, who was also in the coffee shop, told her that I was a lowlife and bad news and to stay away from me. That girl's name was Edith, and she is now my wife and a beautiful Christian woman.

The girls did talk with me and I had coffee with them. They were talking about a young man they had met on a street corner in downtown Kitchener. He had been playing the guitar and preaching from the Bible. They told me that they had sat on a bench and listened to him for a while.

I was about to be hit with one final bolt of supernatural lightning. They told me that after the open air service was finished, the preacher came over and invited them to his church. That was the week prior to me meeting them in the coffee shop. They told me that they had gone to church that night and it had been really different. The people there had been happy, clapping their hands and praising the Lord and raising their arms. A whole band had been on the platform playing gospel music. They were really excited about this church and were talking about going again that Sunday evening.

It amazed me, because as a little boy I had grown up in a fairly traditional church. It hadn't seemed like anybody was happy back then, and not many people had looked like they wanted to be there. People looked at their watches and wished the service was over so they could go home, even though it was only an hour long. Church, to me, was a boring place. A lifeless place, a place where old people went at the end of their lives just waiting to die. I'd never thought young people would go to church and actually enjoy it. I had never seen a happy church before. My friends told me that they were going back to the church that night because they had really enjoyed the service

I so desperately wanted to go with these new friends, but when you're involved in street gangs and motorcycle clubs, it's just not cool to ask if you can go to a church service.

I finished drinking my coffee, got up, and began to walk out of the shop. As I was leaving, God knew my heart. I believe He put it on one of their hearts to invite me to go to the service that night.

"Hochie, how would you like to go to church with us tonight?" one of the girls called out.

I spun around and said yes without even thinking about my answer.

How many times are people desperate to find God, praying for help and seeking the Lord with all their hearts? Yet we don't invite these people to church. We don't have the faith to believe that God may be dealing with them and that they might just come and get saved.

God had been dealing with my heart, and I didn't even recognize Him. He was convicting me of my sin and leading me by the Holy Spirit. Now one of my friends had invited me to a church and I had an opportunity to go and find God. You see, I thought that God lived in church buildings and that was His home. I thought that was the only place you could go to find God or feel God or see Him.

I realize now that God doesn't dwell in temples made with man's hands, but that we are the temple of the Holy Spirit (1 Corinthians 6:19). God lives in us when we invite Him into our hearts. The church is actually the people, not the building. God doesn't want to inhabit brick and mortar; He wants to inhabit the hearts and souls of His creation. The Bible says that God's portion is His people (Deuteronomy 32:9).

After telling them that I would go to church with them, I got on my Harley Davidson and went home. The girls had told me to drop by at about 6:30 p.m. and we would go together.

When I went home, I put on a cleaner pair of dirty pants and a cleaner dirty shirt. I only had blue jeans, old t-shirts, motorcycle boots, and a leather jacket. I had hair down past my shoulders and my face was drawn from years of alcohol abuse. My eyes were sunk into my head from years of wear through the continual abuse of the drugs.

I took my Harley down to church that night and met the girls and one guy who I'd met in the coffee shop earlier that day. I found it strange that God used sinners and not Christians to invite me to church. But God's Word tells us, *"The harvest is truly great, but the labourers are few"* (Luke 10:2). So He used my lost friends to get me to church, as God can do anything to fulfill His will and purpose.

When we walked into the back door, it seemed like everybody was staring at us. I was in my street clothes. The girls were in dresses, but the week before they'd been wearing short shorts and skimpy halter tops. The people all had the same look on their faces; they were smiling from ear to ear. They all began coming towards me and I thought to myself, *What are they going to do?*

At first it seemed that they were going to throw me out and laugh in the process. Perhaps seeing this bike gang member come in his leathers was a good reason to get rid of me. To my surprise, they shook my hand, patted me on the back, and welcomed me. They told me their names and said they were glad to see me. They made me feel like I owned the place. I wasn't someone to despise or someone to get rid of because of the way I looked. To them I was just a sinner who needed to be saved and they were so glad I had come.

The service started and the people began to clap their hands, raise their arms, and praise the Lord. I didn't participate in what I thought was fanatical stuff, but I did enjoy the service. I felt like the air was full of power, the same power I had felt in the back of that ambulance that night in northern Ontario. It was the same power I'd seen in those two young people on the streets of Crystal Beach. It was the power of the Holy Spirit and it filled the air.

People weren't going through rituals and traditions. They really seemed to be enjoying their time praising God. The preacher got up and preached the Word with power and conviction. I don't remember much of what he said, because I was daydreaming and looking around, wondering what these people had in their life that made them so happy. I thought to myself, *I don't know what these people have, but I sure want it.*

After the message was finished, some people stood up and started walking towards the front of the church. I wondered where they were going because I thought the service was over and the door was at the other end of the church.

My friends saw that I was confused and tried to explain what was happening. "Hochie, those people are going up front to get saved."

They had seen this before and they knew what was happening.

Saved? I thought. *What does she mean, saved? I don't know saved. I've never heard about being saved. How do you get saved?*

Suddenly, I heard a voice. It wasn't a human voice, but it was a very real voice and it was speaking into my heart. I heard this voice say, "You need to get saved. You need to get saved. You need to get saved."

I've got to get saved, I thought to myself. *I've got to go down there and get saved with those people. I need to be saved.*

But I didn't know how to get saved and I was afraid to go down there alone.

This was a Spirit-filled Pentecostal church, and they were having an altar call for people to come up and give their lives to the Lord. As a member of the Henchmen, I had learned to be tough and hard.

You weren't supposed to be afraid of anything. Many times I did fearful things—I even faced death—but we never ran from a fight. We could fight with the police, with one another, and with rival gangs. There were times when I had my head beat in, but I wouldn't run.

Yet that night I was terrified to go down to the front of the church alone. I was tough enough to go to prison for police assault, but I wasn't tough enough to make that walk down the aisle to give my life to God.

I asked my friends if they would go down there with me.

They laughed and said, "We're not going down there, never."

I looked up to the ceiling of the church and began to pray to myself quietly. "Oh God, I feel like I'm at the end of my road. I feel that if I leave this church tonight and don't get saved, I'm going to die young and I'll never have another chance. Lord, I want to go down there and get saved, but I'm afraid to go alone."

At that moment, a young man at the front of the church, just a teenager—or maybe he was in his early twenties—jumped up and walked to the back where I was sitting. There were over two hundred people in church that night, but that young person picked on me.

"Do you want to go up there and get saved?" he asked.

"Yes, I do."

"Come on, I'll take you."

I found out later that his name was Josh. He told me that God had spoken to him and told him to go back and get the greasy, long-haired fellow in the leather jacket because he wanted to get saved. Jesus said, *"My sheep hear my voice, and I know them, and they follow me"* (John 10:27). Am I ever glad that young man was a sheep that obeyed the voice of the Lord!

I jumped out into the aisle and went down to the front with a young man I had never met in my life. I left all my friends in the pew behind me.

When I got to the front, the young man left me there alone. I didn't know what to do next. I was standing at the front of the church with a bunch of people on my right and a man and woman on my left. I thought to myself, *I don't know what to do, but I'll watch them and whatever they do, I'll do the same thing, and then I'll get saved.*

I was looking at them, but they weren't doing anything. They were just standing there at the front.

When the preacher came down, his face seemed to shine like an angel. He had that same glow, a radiance of the Holy Spirit on him. As Christians, sometimes we can't see the radiant glow of the Holy Spirit on each other's faces, but the world many times can see that glow.

When the preacher came down to the altar area, he laid his hand on a man's head. He said, "In the name of Jesus," and the man fell on the floor. Then he came to the woman next to me and said, "In the name of Jesus," and she fell on the floor. I was next! I looked at them and I looked at him, and I looked back at them again. I thought to myself; *Is this how you get saved? This guy kills you and then God takes you?* I didn't know what he had done to them. I'd never been in a church like this before. They had fallen down under the power of the Holy Spirit.

In John 18:26, when Jesus was in the Garden of Gethsemane and an entire band of Roman soldiers came to arrest Him, Jesus said, "Who are you looking for?"

"Jesus of Nazareth," they answered.

"I am He."

After saying those words, the entire Roman army fell to the ground under the power of God. I believe Jesus did that so the Roman army and the world would know that they hadn't taken Him by force. He had the power to knock them to the ground with a few simple words. He freely went with them to give His life for our sins.

In the book of Revelation, John fell down like a dead man when Jesus appeared to him. In the Old Testament, when the glory of God would fall on the Israelite camp, the people would fall in the doors of their tents, prostrate before the Lord. Paul the apostle fell to the ground on the Damascus road. You see, when the power of the Holy Spirit comes on you, sometimes it takes away your physical strength. You fall down in the presence of God.

Suddenly, I heard a voice whispering to me, but it was not God's voice. It wasn't like the voice telling me to get saved. This was more of a cynical, evil voice, but it was very real. I heard something whisper into my mind: "You've got to get out of this church now. You must leave right away because this is a holy-roller church."

Oh no, I thought. *I'm in a holy-roller church. I've heard about these people. They roll on the floors, swing from the lights, and jump out windows.*

My uncle used to call them the gooks. These were crazy, religious people. How had I ever gotten into a holy-roller church? What's really amazing is that I eventually attended the church where he used to call the people gooks. I was also the one to lead my uncle to the Lord when he was in the hospital dying of an incurable disease.

I'm not going to roll on the floor for anybody. I'm a member of the Henchmen Motorcycle Club. I'm tough. I've punched people's lights out in the past. I'll punch out the lights of this preacher if he tries to push me down. I'm getting out of this nuthouse and I'm never coming back again.

But God had different plans for me. If God says you're going to roll, you're going to roll. You don't have to fall on the floor to get saved, but it sure helps for God to knock you down a couple of notches when you think you're bigger and tougher than the Lord. As E.V. Hill once said, "Your arms are too short to box with God."

The preacher didn't pray for me right away like he did the others. He asked me why I had come to church. I was going to say "I don't know," but other words came out of my mouth instead. They were not even in my mind. I said, "I'm here to find Jesus." I actually startled myself and thought, *Why did I say that?* God took the words from my heart and put them in my mouth.

You see, I was searching for God, but Jesus said, *"I am the way, the truth, and the life: no man cometh unto the Father, but by me"* (John 14:6). When you're searching for God, the only way to get to Him is through Jesus. He is the only begotten Son who came from heaven to save us from our sins.

The preacher then said. "Do you have the faith?"

"I think so."

He looked at me but didn't say anything.

Then I heard the voice of God. It was so clear. I heard Him say, "What do you mean you think so? Either you believe or you don't."

It's either hot or cold, in or out, yes or no. There's no such thing as being half a Christian or living in a grey area. You are either born again or you're lost and going to hell. Jesus said, *"Except a man be born again, he cannot [enter] the kingdom of God"* (John 3:3). You cannot be born again unless you have faith to believe that Jesus Christ died on the cross, that He rose again from the dead and therefore has power to give you eternal life.

I looked at the preacher and thought to myself, *I believe.* And then I said it out loud. "I believe."

He reached out his hand, but he never even touched me.

"In the name of Jesus," he said, and I fell to the floor under the power of Almighty God.

When I hit the floor. I tried to get up but couldn't. I struggled desperately. I could barely lift my head; my arms wouldn't move, my legs wouldn't move. It was like God had His foot on me and He was saying, "Stay there, tough guy, until I'm done with you."

My friends saw me fall down and they were amazed.

"We thought for sure you would come up swinging and punch that preacher out for pushing you down there," they said to me after.

But he didn't push me down; it was the power of God that knocked me prostrate onto the floor. When I realized I couldn't get up, I just lay my head back and looked up at the ceiling of the church. I said to God, *I don't know what's happening here. I don't understand. But whatever it is, I accept it.*

That night, nobody prayed a sinner's prayer with me. Nobody read scripture to me. Nobody told me how to get saved. God, in His sovereignty, began to open the eyes of my understanding. While lying on the floor of that church, I began to see that the problem wasn't the drugs, violence, sex, or all the horrible things we were doing. Those are outward things caused from an inward problem in our hearts. God began to show me that my heart was dirty; my motives, my attitude, my desires were all wrong. Jesus Christ said that sin comes from the heart. It doesn't come from outside the body; it comes from within (Matthew 15:18–20). He also said that we should first clean up the inside of the cup (the heart), then the outside would just naturally be clean (Matthew 23:25–26).

When Jesus Christ comes into our lives, He cleans up our hearts; He changes us from the inside out. You can wash a pig, you can dress it up and put a ribbon around its neck, and you can even perfume the animal, but it's still a pig. You can take a bike gang member and you can put a suit on him and shave him and clean his hair and even take him to church, but in his heart he's still a bike gang member.

The problem with humanity is that we have evil, sinful hearts from birth. That's because we are born into sin and shaped in iniquity, as David said in Psalm 51:5. It's natural for us to want to do things wrong because that's in our blood. We know how to sin. So Jesus Christ came to set the captives free. He came to clean us up, change us from the inside out, and give us a brand new heart.

That night, while I was on the floor of that church, something wonderful happened. I felt the power of God. I had only experienced it on the outside before, but now it poured into my body and into my heart and life. I could literally feel Jesus Christ come into me, and I could feel demons going out of my body. I felt clean, as if pure water was flowing through my soul, and dirty, muddy water was pushed out. I really believe that I was demonized. When Jesus Christ came into my heart, demons and devils were forced to leave. Christ and Satan have no fellowship together. Light and dark cannot cohabitate. When Christ comes in, the devil must leave.

I was supernaturally saved by the grace of God through faith in Jesus Christ, but it wasn't until a couple of weeks later that I realized what had actually happened to me. I found out in the Word of God.

For by grace are ye saved through faith; and that not of yourselves: it is the gift of God: not of works, lest any man should boast. (Ephesians 2:8–9)

I looked up at the ceiling of the church as this power flowed through my body. The ceiling of the church lit up whiter and brighter than any snow I had ever seen. At that point, I heard what sounded like angels singing around the throne. At first I thought it was the people in the church, but somebody told me later that I probably did hear angels singing. The Bible says that all the angels of heaven rejoice around the throne of God when just one sinner comes home and gets saved (Luke 15:10).

You don't have to feel anything to become a Christian. You don't have to have a dramatic experience like I did. I wasn't saved because I got knocked to the floor or because I felt God's power flowing through me. I was saved merely because I believed on the Lord Jesus Christ.

Some people don't feel anything, yet their salvation is just as real as mine. I didn't want to get off the floor. I enjoyed the power and presence of God so much. But all of a sudden, I felt like my body was released. I knew that I could get off the floor. I got up and found that there was no strength in my legs. I made for the nearest pew and sat down.

Then I heard that evil voice again speak to me: "You fool, you idiot. How could you ever roll around on the floor of a church like that? Your friends, the Henchmen, your family are all going to laugh you out of town once they hear you were lying on the floor of a church. You're finished."

What have I done? I wondered.

The devil will try to steal away the seed that God puts into your heart (Matthew 13:18–19). He will try to destroy the very salvation God has given you because you called on the Lord.

God knew that I doubted as I sat alone in that pew. The same young man from earlier came back and sat beside me. "Don't doubt," he said.

How did this guy know I had been doubting? Was he in my head? God had told him to go over and talk to me and tell me not to doubt but to keep believing. He told me that the Christian walk wouldn't always be easy. He shared with me that I would still have to face some storms in life, but that if I trusted God, He would see me through every battle. As he was talking, the doubts faded away.

Then a woman at the back of the church began to cry. The whole church grew quiet as she got up and said, "I want to give a testimony." The pastor told her to go ahead. When she had opened her eyes that morning, she'd seen an angel from God standing beside her bed. The angel spoke to her and said, "God has chosen you as a vessel of prayer, but you are not to ask who you are praying for. You are to pray until you believe that your prayer has been answered." The angel then left the room. Through tear-filled eyes, this woman told the church, "I got out of bed and I began to pray for somebody I do not know. I prayed all morning until I felt released that God had answered my prayer."

After she finished giving that testimony, I felt the Lord speak to my heart one more time: "Dale, I got that lady to pray for you tonight so I could bring you in here. This is the day of your decision. This is the day of your salvation. Now you either accept me or you reject me."

At that point, I knew that my life had changed and there was no turning back. I jumped off that pew and began running around the church. I think I shook every hand in the building. I said, "I'm a Christian, I'm a Christian. I'm saved, I'm saved."

I grabbed one lady's hand and said, "May the glory and the power of God shine from within me for everybody to see."

I was only saved for a couple of minutes and already I was beginning to prophesy. Henchmen don't talk that kind of language. We could cuss the wallpaper off a wall, as we had very foul, wicked mouths. But already the Holy Spirit was starting to change my conversation. My friends saw me running around the church shaking hands and telling people that I was Christian. A couple of them thought that maybe I had gone crazy and lost my mind. They went outside and lit cigarettes to calm their nerves.

I came busting out the front doors of the church. "You've got to get it, you've got to get it."

"Get what?" they asked.

"I don't know, but you've got to get it." I didn't even know how to tell them about being saved or how I'd gotten saved. I just knew I was saved!

"That's good," they said to me. "You keep it, because we don't want it."

I went straight home from that church service and busted in the front door of our house. My mother and one of her boarders were there with my brother, president of the Henchmen. They were watching television.

"Guess what happened tonight?" I asked. "Guess what happened!"

They all jumped up and looked at me. "What? Was it a beating? A stabbing? Did somebody get shot? Was there an accident? Quick, tell us what happened."

"I was lying on the floor of a church—"

My brother just shook his head and lay back down on the couch. "He's stoned again."

"Dale," my mother started, "what are you talking about, you were lying on the floor of a church?"

"Mom, I don't know what happened, but tonight I'm a Christian."

"But Dale, you've always been a Christian."

My mom was such a beautiful woman with such a loving heart that she just couldn't see the bad in me.

"Mom, I beat heads, I've shot dope, I've been in drunken brawls, in and out of jail, I take God's name in vain and swear. How can you say I'm a Christian?"

Just like a loving mother, she said, "Oh Dale, you weren't all that bad."

My mom was a good woman and she even went to church for many years. The problem was that she never knew Jesus Christ as her personal Lord and Saviour. Nobody had ever told her that she had to have a personal salvation. She used to say, "When I die, I hope I'll go to heaven." You need to know before you die that you're going to heaven (1 John 5:13). You need to know that Jesus Christ has forgiven you from your sins and saved you for all eternity.

The next priority in my life was to be a witness to my family and friends and lead as many of them to Christ as possible. I was just a new Christian myself, but I began to witness and share Christ in any way I could. It didn't take long for all of my friends and the members of the Henchmen to find out that I had gotten religion. I didn't blame them for making fun of me and putting me down. I would have done the same thing had one of them become a Christian, and I would have remained as a member of the Henchmen. But God gave me many opportunities to share Christ with them and tell them how God had changed my life, how He had forgiven me for all my sins. Praise the Lord!

One night a member of the club called me on the phone and asked me to come and pick him up at the clubhouse. He said he was too drunk to ride his motorcycle home. I drove over to the clubhouse in my car and walked up to the front door. He opened the door and told me to come in because he wasn't finished with his beer. I walked into the clubhouse only to see many of the friends I had once rode with and partied with in the club. There was about twelve of them there that night. I wasn't afraid, because these people were no different than me or anybody else. I also knew that God was with me and I was not alone.

They made a circle around me and began to make fun of me, saying things like "Jesus freak," "Holy-roller," and "Bible-puncher." These are some of the things people say when you give your life to Jesus and become a Christian. I didn't let it bother me because I really wanted to be a good witness for these guys, hoping that maybe some of them would eventually turn their lives around.

They didn't try to force me to do anything I didn't want—no drugs, no drinking. They were just making fun of me, but they also asked questions. "Hochie, how did you flip so fast? How did you go from this to that? From bike gangs to religion? Did you get some drugs stuck in your brain? What went wrong with you?"

I told those guys that I was no different than them and no better than anyone else. I was just a sinner saved by grace, and they were sinners not saved by grace. I told them that God loved them just as much as He loved me, but that they needed to give their lives to Him.

One member came up to me and said, "I don't believe there is a God."

"The Bible tells us that a fool would say in his heart that there is no God." That was from Psalm 14:1.

"Are you calling me a fool?" he asked.

"No, God is. You need to talk to Him."

He just turned around and walked away.

Another member came up to me whose name was Psycho. He really was the psycho of the club. He was kind of crazy and he had that crazy look in his eyes. My wife was always just a little bit afraid of him.

"Hochie, you're nuts," Psycho said.

"Yeah, Psycho, but at least I'm screwed onto the right bolt."

I left the clubhouse that night without any of them trying to hurt me. They were my friends, and I left the club in good standing. I was a model member and they really wanted me back in the club. It probably helped that my brother was president of the gang, and my mom bordered Henchmen in her house.

One of the things I found difficult was coming home from church on a Sunday. My brother Mac and the other members would have bike gang meetings in the front room of our house. I was the only Christian up against forty of my friends. They were constantly in and out of my residence. However, I didn't care what it cost me; I was going to be a good Christian witness. I might have been the only chance some of these guys would ever have to see the love of God and see how Jesus Christ could really change somebody. They used to laugh at me and tell me that it wouldn't last. They said it was only a phase, a fad. They were wrong. It has lasted for many years and I have never turned my back on Jesus Christ.

I came into the house one afternoon while they were having a club meeting in my mom's living room.

"Hey, the rev is here," they said.

I had begun to learn some scriptures as Christians taught and instructed me in areas of the Bible. I was excited and anxious to try and use some of my newfound knowledge on them. I guess I was actually trying to be a little bit too religious.

"You know what?" I said. "I love you guys. And the Bible says that if you want me to go one mile with you, I'll go two. If you want my coat, I'll give you my shirt also. Whatever belongs to me belongs to you. What's mine is yours."

I wasn't really speaking with much wisdom; I was just trying to quote a scripture.

One of the members got up and came over to me. "Did you say anything that belongs to you belongs to me?"

"That's right."

He then said to me, "I want your Harley Davidson."

I had a full-dressed Harley with a custom paint job that was worth a bit of money. I really didn't think when I quoted that scripture that anybody would ask for my motorcycle. I had backed myself into a corner, and at that moment I knew I had spoken unwisely. I had only done it to impress my friends.

All those bike gang members sat there looking at me, waiting to see what I would do. I knew that if told them I wouldn't give up my motorcycle, I would be a liar and they wouldn't listen to anything else I had to say. I also knew that if I gave away my motorcycle, I'd be losing the only thing that I owned of any value.

It's either my bike or my witness, I told myself.

"Go get a pen," I said to the guy. I then pulled my wallet out of my pocket and removed the ownership document for my bike. "The motorcycle is yours. I'm signing it over to you right now. You've just got yourself a Harley Davidson motorcycle."

The souls of those young men were far more important to me than the bike. I would rather lose my Harley than have those young men lost in hell for all eternity.

He looked at me for a moment and then just waved his hand in front of my face and said, "Ahhh, forget it. I just wanted to see if you would do it."

He then walked back to sit down.

In my heart I was saying, *Glory to God, Hallelujah, thank You, Jesus, praise the Lord.* God had gotten me out of a mess. I was very careful after that to use the Word of God only as the Holy Spirit directed me.

Chapter 8

MY BROTHER AND MY MOTHER

MY BROTHER

My brother's name is Richard, but we always called him Mac. Today he is also a born-again Christian. He joined the club after I did and eventually became president of the organization. What you're about to read are his experiences, in his own words.

* * *

I joined the Henchmen a few months after my brother. Many of my motorcycle buddies were also joining up with that club. One particular member put a lot of pressure on us to become members, so finally I gave in and got my patch.

We felt at that time that we were invincible, full of spit and vinegar and that nothing could hurt us or stop us. The thing I liked about hanging out with these guys was riding my motorcycle. I always enjoyed riding, but there was also the partying aspect and the women. I don't understand why, but it seemed like a lot of young girls and women were drawn to this lifestyle, and that mesmerized me. The girls came from all walks of life—from poor families as well as rich families, from everyday average families to families that were high up in society, it didn't seem to matter. I would venture to say that we had some of the prettiest girls in the region on the back of our motorcycles, yet we treated them very badly.

I relished the tough image like a lot of the other guys. There was an aspect of pride and male ego to it, but you couldn't see it at the time. You can become very egotistical and hard, because you think it's "all for one and one for all." You really believe that nothing will ever go wrong and that you can do no wrong. I found out in my club years that when times really got tough, your friends were not always there for you. Sometimes the men you thought would stand with you the tightest were the ones who gave you the least support.

Fear is a terrible thing when it begins to take hold of you, especially in matters of life and death. I dated a girl in the club whose father was a born-again Christian. As a matter of fact, he was a very stanch kind of Christian man, but filled with a lot of love and compassion. She was raised in a strict Christian home and her dad was Spirit-filled. She ended up sitting on the back of my motorcycle and becoming what we called "my old lady."

I didn't like striking for the club because sometimes you had to do some crazy things that might have gotten you into trouble or created major problems. When I was club president, I had to stop things that some of the members wanted to do to the newest members. They didn't like that I tried to run the club from a common sense approach, which seemed impossible, because at times I worked with guys who had wild ideas and were extraordinarily dysfunctional.

My years in the club started good, but it deteriorated very quickly. I ended up living a very brutal life of hell. We even had a lawyer working on the inside for us. He would come and party at our clubhouse, yet stand in court and defend us before a judge. Sometimes rounders and civilians came to the clubhouse to party with us—at least, that's what we called them. But when things went bad, they tended to get dragged into the trouble along with the members. Some of them even ended up in prison.

Some members were arrested for charges such as murder, rape, police assault, and various drug-related charges. In the years I was in the gang, there was a lot of partying and fighting but it had not yet entered the phase of organized crime that bike gangs are known for today.

The Henchmen were known as a club that went around smashing up the city and fighting. Sometimes our parties became brutal. One night in the Maryhill Hotel, one of our members got thrown around. Some of us went from the clubhouse to the hotel to even the score, and we ended up wrecking the hotel. On our way back into town, we passed the police who were heading to the hotel. A number of members were arrested after that ordeal. My own brother Dale was arrested that night, although he had nothing to do with that melee. He was simply riding down Victoria Street in Kitchener and the police pulled him over and saw that his name was Hoch. They thought they were arresting me, because I happened to be president at the time.

One night we decided to go out to a different hotel in a little town by the name of Baden. When we walked in the door, the whole hotel grew quiet because we were sporting our colours. Everybody was looking at us. I remember the bartender pulled out a baseball bat and set it on top of the counter. There were a lot of farmers and country boys in the hotel that night. We knew they weren't going to let us wreck their hotel. I used a common sense approach, turned around, and said to the members, "We're not staying in this hotel. We're leaving." And we walked out.

Because Dale has already talked a lot about what happened through the years of the club, I would like to talk about how the club started coming apart during the years I was president—and how it finally came to an end.

I first saw things starting to come apart at a field party where something really bad went down with a young girl. Suddenly, we saw the riot squad coming through the field with the local police force. Others came up the laneway with full riot gear. We knew that if we did anything to raise a hand against them, this would basically be the end for us. We were all arrested and taken to jail that day. Some guys were charged and booked, and the rest were let go.

Things started to change for me personally when I went to visit someone in Kingston Penitentiary. Two of our members were doing time. When I walked inside and saw the gun towers and jail cells spiralling up to the ceiling, I thought to myself, *I don't want to sit in here for the rest of my life.*

What I didn't fully realize at the time is that I had a brother who was already a Christian, and he was praying for me and praying that God would bring this club to an end. Little did I know that it would happen sooner than I thought.

The worst of my years in the club was when we had a gang war. Some of our members were giving members from a rival club a rough time in the hotels. It began to escalate from there. This is how gang wars begin and how people end up getting killed. We had a visit at our clubhouse from some members that came from different chapters across the province. They told us that we needed to cool it, but nobody listened.

It had escalated to a point where one of our members had an encounter with a rival club member. It ended up in a fight and they ripped off his patch and brought it to the clubhouse. When you rip off a patch from a member of another club, you might as well have taken their life; that patch is something they must defend with their life. The code was death before dishonour. This was the beginning of the last gang war for our club, and it became quite violent.

The police were involved, as well as a SWAT team. Things got out of hand very fast. A sensational story was written in papers all across Canada about a raid on our clubhouse during the time of that gang war. The police broke the windows during the raid and shotguns came through the openings. It seemed as if the guys holding the guns were shaking because they were so pumped on adrenaline. It was a very dangerous time. They turned German Sheppard dogs loose in the clubhouse, and they bit many of the members and some of their girlfriends. Then they separated the girls and the men and took us to jail. They took us down into the corridor in the basement. One of the police snapped a photo of us kneeling on the floor with our hands cuffed behind our backs while a German Sheppard was turned loose to bite us at will. The officer didn't like what was coming down and sent the photo to a local newspaper, *The Kitchener-Waterloo Record*. From there it went all across Canada.

As a result of that incident, the tactical squad was disbanded and the police chief was dismissed. We as a club had to go after the police for that one because it was the police taking the law into their own hands, which is wrong even when dealing with a bike gang. That particular raid didn't stop the gang wars, though, or slow us down. Things spiralled downward from there. It was exceptionally dangerous for me, because usually rivals would go after the top guys to try to demoralize the club.

One night I came out and found that all the tires on my car had been slit, and there was a knife stuck into the driver's seat. I found a note on the steering wheel saying this person wanted his patch back. What really brought things to a head was fighting with the police and this rival club at the same time. It became overwhelming.

After an intense meeting at our clubhouse, we decided to return the crest to the other club. Myself and two other guys dropped it off that night. We all realized we were in a really dangerous position. We pretended that we had guns, with one member putting his hand in his jacket as if to draw a weapon. We did that because we thought the other club was packing weapons.

Not long after that, we decided to end the club, as many of the members no longer had the desire to continue living this kind of lifestyle. Some of our members were married and had children. They just decided that enough was enough.

Dale had witnessed to me many different times through the years, but I remained a Henchman four years after he left and became a Christian. There were nights when I got mad at him and told him to leave me alone or I would beat his head in. I may have believed some of what he was saying, but I didn't want to admit it.

When I was alone or with my Christian father-in-law, I used to watch Christian programs. One night in my bedroom, and he said something that touched my heart.

"Yeah," I said to God that night. "I need that."

Not long after that experience, I spent an evening with my brother Dale. He then went home and told his wife that I was saved. She asked him how he knew I was saved, and Dale answered that I *looked* saved.

He then took me out for supper at Taco Bell and asked me straight if I had given my life to the Lord. I told him what I'd said in my bedroom.

"Does that make you saved?" I asked.

He said, "Yes."

For an hour, we talked about the Bible and scriptures. That was the beginning of my Christian life.

Shortly thereafter, my wife recommitted her life to the Lord. She had been a Christian in her early years but had backslidden. Today we are a Christian family, I have a beautiful Christian wife, and I have lovely Christian kids; a couple of them are married and we have become grandparents.

MY MOTHER

My mother came to know Jesus as her Saviour in the first year after I came to know the Lord. It wasn't until many years later that my brother Mac accepted Jesus.

On different days I witnessed to her and told her she needed Jesus Christ as her Saviour. She would sometimes plug her ears and say, "I don't want to hear it." I would chase her with my Bible from the living room to the dining room, then to the kitchen, trying to show her scriptures and convince her that she needed to be saved.

My mom had been raised in a very traditional church and believed that going through confirmation and being baptized as a baby was enough to get you into heaven. She admitted that she wasn't sure if she was really going to heaven. She only hoped she would go there when she died. She used to say, "Nobody knows until they get there." But the Bible says we know that we have passed from death to life because we have God's love (1 John 3:14). One day my mother finally gave in, admitted that she needed Jesus Christ, and became a Christian.

When you take a very loving woman like my mom and get her saved and filled with the Holy Ghost, the devil has a big problem. My mom witnessed to anybody who would listen to her. One time a wrong number phoned the house and my mom talked to that person about the Lord for two hours.

Another time, my mom and I were serving the Lord but my brother was still involved in the gang. My mom then answered a telephone call and the person on the other end began to scream at her and tell her she was a wicked, good-for-nothing woman. He said that her sons were wicked and that every one of us was going to hell. He then said that he was going to help send us to hell, and that the next time she stepped out on the front porch he was going to blow her away.

My mom responded in a very kind and loving voice: "Oh, you wouldn't want to do that. Jesus wouldn't like it." With that, there was a click and the phone went dead. I'm sure it wasn't the response the caller was expecting to hear.

We need to sincerely ask for forgiveness and believe on the Lord Jesus Christ. The Bible tells us that there's a lamb for a household. I believe in household salvation! God brought my entire family from gang wars and guns to Christ. That is what happens when the Lord thunders from heaven.

My mother never allowed drugs or stolen goods in her house, but she always allowed us and our friends to stay, no matter what we had done and no matter how bad our situation was. I realize now, looking back, that a lot of the guys I lived with, drank with, fought with, and went to jail with were just looking for acceptance and love. That's exactly what my mother gave to every member of the club. They were looking for somebody to care about them so they could feel special. She just loved people, she loved life, and love *"covers the multitude of sins"* (1 Peter 4:8).

Every one of the members of our club treated my mom with respect. They all called her Ma! Many of the rounders, street people, and girls called her Ma because she treated everyone like her own children. At Christmas time, my mom would put out extra plates around the tables because people would come in off the streets and out of the hotels from the clubhouse with nowhere to go for Christmas dinner. They had nobody to spend Christmas with, so they would come in and spend it with my mom. My mom would feed every one of them and wouldn't turn anybody away. At Christmas time, we would sometimes have five, six, or seven other people sitting around the table having dinner with us.

One situation totally amazed me, and I got to see how the power of love can change a person. Two gang members came to my house one day for a visit, and they were pretty rough-looking boys. One of them was Grizzly, who I spoke of earlier. They walked into the front door of my mom's house. They didn't knock, because the door was always open. They had just come from the hotel and had finished drinking a few pitchers of bear.

"Hey Ma, make us a sandwich," one of them said. "We're hungry."

My mother was having a little bit of a bad time that day. As they walked into her dining room, she stood before those two big bikers, put out her finger, and began to scold them. "You two guys are becoming a couple of lazy, good-for-nothing bums. You sit at the hotel all morning, you drink beer, you come back to eat my food, and then you go back to the hotel and drink for the rest of the day. If you were real men, you would make something of your lives and you'd go out and get yourselves a job."

With that, the two of them turned around and walked out of the house. Nobody talked to bikers that way! My mom thought to herself. *Well, maybe I was too hard on them. Maybe I shouldn't have said that.*

They came back half an hour later and walked into the dining room again.

"Ma, make us that sandwich," they said. "We got ourselves a job and we're hungry."

Because of my mom's scolding, the two of them had gone up the street a couple of blocks to a factory called Domtar Packaging. They'd gone in and asked if there were jobs available. They were hired immediately and told to start the next morning. The explanation they gave to the club was, "Ma told us to get a job, so we got a job!"

Not only did those two men get a job, but they kept those jobs for many years, just because my mom cared enough to give them a little scolding in love. People seem to forget that people in street gangs or bike gangs are still human beings. They're no different than any other person in society, except they've been caught up in a wilder lifestyle, living on the edge and doing things the average person wouldn't do. Whether it's violence, criminal activity, or just telling a lie, sin is sin.

Every one of us will pay the price for our sins if we don't give our lives over to Jesus Christ before we pass into eternity. I thank God today that Jesus Christ is no respecter of persons. I've always said, and continue to say today, that the ground at the foot of the cross is level. Nobody is any better than anyone else. We all need a Saviour, from the halls of our government to the gutters of society where drug addicts and prostitutes make their living.

Many of the members of our club, and rounders from the hotels, would bring gifts to mom to say thanks for loving us. After she became a Christian, her love became a tremendous threat to the powers of hell.

When my mom passed away, five hundred people came to the funeral home to say goodbye. Many of them were bikers, street people, prostitutes, and drug addicts. That shows the power of love!

Chapter 9

APPOINTMENTS FROM ABOVE

After becoming a Christian, I was filled with the power of the Holy Spirit, just as the people were at Pentecost in Acts 2. I began to see the gifts of the Holy Spirit manifest in my life, and God began to lead me into supernatural encounters. I had divine appointments with the Lord and certain individuals.

From the first year I was a Christian, I felt the call of God on my life to ministry. The first place God took me was back to the streets—the highways, the byways, the hedges, and the gutters, to reach the drug addicts, the homosexuals, the prostitutes, the alcoholic, and the criminals of society.

> *And the lord said unto the servant, Go out into the highways and hedges, and compel them to come in, that my house may be filled. For I say unto you, That none of those men which were bidden shall taste of my supper.* (Luke 14:23–24)

One day I was sitting at home in the dining room and heard a knock at the door. I went to answer and saw two men standing on the porch. They introduced themselves and said that they were from *The Kitchener-Waterloo Record*. They had heard that I'd been in the Henchmen Motorcycle Club and that I had "gotten religion." They were wondering if they could come in and interview me. They wanted to do a story on bike gangs in the region and wanted to include my story about becoming a Christian. I agreed to the interview and to take some pictures, but only if they printed exactly what I said and didn't change my words.

During the interview, I was able to share not only about my own personal life and the destructive path I had been on, but also about giving my life to Jesus Christ. I told them how God had changed my heart and my life and had called me to the ministry.

The paper did a full-page article, and the Henchmen where the featured club due to the fact they were considered the worst. The paper had a picture of the bikers riding in a funeral procession after the death of one of our members. I was actually riding in that funeral procession. One-quarter of the page was reserved for my story. They put a before and after picture and printed exactly what I had told them to print.

God gave me the opportunity to witness to the entire region. *The Record* had a readership of about three hundred thousand people, so in one day I was able to witness to thousands of people. Amazingly, it was absolutely free advertising. I called it my gospel tract from heaven, as I could never have afforded that kind of publication.

Another time, a young man was saved. He was a good friend of mine, a walking Bible. If anyone talked about a scripture, he could quote book, chapter, and verse without even looking. He had amazing recall. However, that young man backslid and began to hang out with drug addicts and people living in a street commune. I heard that he was at a specific house, so I went looking for him, to see if I could convince him to come back to the Lord. When I walked up the walkway to the house, all the young people ran inside except for one person. When they saw my Bible, they had thought I was Jehovah witness.

I walked up to the one remaining guy.

"Are you Jehovah's Witness?" he asked.

"No," I said. "I'm a Christian."

With that, he called out to the young people inside and said, "Come on out. It's okay."

It always amazes me that they were afraid of a Jehovah's Witness, but they weren't afraid of a Christian. They came out on the porch and began making fun of me and trying to get me to smoke a joint or pop a pill. I told them I was high on Jesus and that I didn't need that high anymore. I didn't condemn them or put them down, I just shared Christ with them and told them about God's love.

I asked them if my friend was there, and they said he wasn't. But they were lying. I found out later that he was inside hiding.

After I left the house and was driving away, I felt the Holy Spirit say to me, "You've got to go back to that house. You're not done there yet."

I pulled over and prayed to make sure it was God speaking. "God, is that you speaking to me? Am I supposed to go back?"

With that, I felt myself turning the car around, almost as if the Lord took control. Back I went to the house. The same young people were still out on the porch, still toking up and drinking.

I walked up the front steps and a young man came out of the crowd. His name was Matt, and he hadn't been there the first time.

"Are you that religious nut who was here a few minutes ago?" he asked.

"Well, I was here a few minutes ago."

"I'm glad you came back, because I want to talk to you." With that, he began to mock me, but he also asked very serious questions. His brother had been killed in an automobile accident a few months before and he was very bitter and angry with God. Yet I sensed that he was searching for answers and reaching out to find out why, and to see if God cared for him.

I began to share some scripture with him and what God wanted to do in his life. After a time of talking with him, I left the house again and went home. God then spoke to me about going to see Matt a second time and sharing the gospel with him.

When we think we're on a supernatural assignment to help one person, we're actually sometimes directed by God to reach somebody else. Just like the Apostle Paul with the Macedonia call. God changed his direction and sent him to a different place.

I went back to the house, but Matt was gone and nobody knew where he was. I began searching the streets for him. I talked to everybody who knew him, but nobody knew where he was. He had just disappeared. The more I looked for him, the more God kept saying to me, "You've got to find Matt. You've got to find him and tell him about my love."

After three months of searching, I couldn't find him and God was still dealing with me.

Finally, one night I prayed, *God, I don't know where Matt is, but You do. If You find him, I will talk to him.*

The next Sunday, while teaching a youth Sunday school class, I had a couple of absentees. The girl in the office had written down the names and phone numbers of the absentees and gave me the list to go home and phone them after church. I went home that afternoon and sat down to phone one of the young people. His name was Jed.

A young man answered the phone and I said, "Hi Jed, is that you?"

"No, it's not Jed."

"Well, then who is this?"

He replied, "It's Matt."

I almost fell out of the chair. I later realized that the girl in the office had taken the phone number of my Sunday school student and gotten one digit wrong. I had phoned a wrong number and found Matt, the person I'd been looking to find for months. Only a supernatural God could do that. The chances of that happening are maybe one in a billion. I told him that I had been looking for him for three months to tell him that God loves him. I explained how I'd found him through a wrong number. I shared with him that God had his number and wanted him to come to Jesus Christ and surrender his life. I'm always amazed at what God does and how He deals with people who are searching for Him and looking for answers.

I had another experience one night around 11:00 p.m. The phone rang, and when I answered it a voice on the other end said, "Hi. I'd like to come over and see you. You don't know who I am, but I want to come and talk to you."

I felt the Holy Spirit speak to my heart and say, *Let him come. I have sent him.*

I told him to come over and I gave him the address.

Not long after, I heard knocking at the door. This young man came in and I took him into my office. He sat down and began to talk. I asked how he'd gotten my phone number.

"How do you know me?" I asked.

"I'm from the Canadian Armed Forces, and I'm depressed and I want to die. I have a revolver in my pocket. I was going to take the bus to the end of the line on the outskirts of the city. Then I was going to go out into a field and put a bullet in my head."

He shared about how he had been sitting on the back of the bus waiting for the trip to end so he could end his life. All of a sudden, power began to surround his body. It was a power he had never experienced before. The power pulled him up out of his seat. He didn't want to get off the bus, so he tried not to get up; he actually hung on to the seat, but the power was stronger than him. He was supernaturally pulled up, and that power took him from the back of the bus to the front.

Next to the driver's seat was a garbage pile which had been swept up from things the passengers had left behind. He reached down and put his hand into this pile of garbage and grabbed a piece of paper. The driver and everybody on the bus looked at him as if he was crazy. He then walked back to his seat and sat down.

When everybody quit looking at him, he opened his hand to see what he was holding. It was a gospel tract. He began to read the message of God's love. After reading the tract, he noticed that there was a phone number on the back. He got off the bus and went to a phone booth. Then he phoned the number on the back of the tract, and that's how he got to my house.

I was able to lead that young man to Jesus Christ and stop him from taking his own life. Rather than committing suicide, he gained a reason to live. If God can use a jackass in the Bible to preach to the wicked prophet Balaam, He can also use a garbage pile to bring somebody to the saving knowledge of Jesus Christ.

Some of my Christian friends and I would walk the streets of Kitchener-Waterloo, as well as outlying cities such as Toronto and London looking for street kids. We wanted to bring them hope from a life torn apart by sin and shame. We would go into pool halls, hotels, and arcades. We'd go into back alleys where young people were hiding out and doing drugs. The Bible tells us that the love of God casts out fear because fear has torment (1 John 4:18). We never seemed to be afraid, because we knew that *"greater is he that is in you, than he that was in the world"* (1 John 4:4).

One night I felt the Lord leading me to a specific hotel, but first I went and got a Christian friend to go with me; Jesus always sent the disciples two at a time. My friend looked at me with wide eyes, wondering if I was crazy. This hotel was probably considered the lowest hotel of the entire region. When every other hotel in the city kicked you out, this place would take you in. It's the hotel where all the bikers, drug addicts, and prostitutes made their home.

We took our Bibles so people would know we weren't going in there to drink and do drugs and party. We were there on a mission from God.

When we walked in the front door, everybody stared up into the corner. When I turned to look at what they were watching, I saw that it was a Billy Graham crusade. God had brought us there at the perfect moment. While Billy Graham was preaching on television, we went around from table to table putting tracts by each person, telling them the way of salvation.

God's timing is so perfect. Had we come in before or after, it could have been a very dangerous situation! When we worked our way to the back of the room, we came to one table and a man began to yell at us and swear. He was drunk and he looked very angry.

"What are you doing here?" he said. "Get out! Christians don't belong in these places."

I thought to myself, *It's funny that he should know Christians don't belong in a hotel.*

I told him that we hadn't come to drink, but that we were on God's business. The Lord had sent us to the hotel.

"God would never send you into this hotel. You're a liar!" He was very loud and everybody in the room began to look at us and get agitated.

"I'm not a liar," I said. "I can show you right here in the Bible where God told us to come into this hotel." I opened up the Bible and showed him the verse that says, *"And he said unto them, Go ye into all the world, and preach the gospel to every creature"* (Mark 16:5). "Sir, some creatures never come out of these places, so we've got to come in."

With that, he became extraordinarily angry and began to curse louder. He pulled back his fist to punch me in the mouth. I could see my teeth were about to be on the floor, not to mention that he was getting everybody else worked up. I could feel the tension rising as he drew back his fist to punch me in the face. I didn't know it, but my friend had already made a beeline for the door and was waiting for me at the exit.

I only had time to whisper a little prayer: "Jesus, help!"

At that moment, as the man was cussing and before he was able to hit me, his false teeth flew about an inch out of his lips and turned sideways. Then he sucked them back into his mouth and began choking on them. While he was trying to get his teeth back in, I had time to get over to the exit where my friend was waiting. I turned around and saw that the whole room was looking us.

I began to preach one of my first public sermons. "You know, God sent us in here tonight to tell you that He loves you and that He'll save you from your sins. You need to call on Jesus Christ, and you need to ask God to forgive you. God will not turn anybody away who calls from a sincere heart."

With that, we turned and walked out the door.

God gave me a pulpit on the street. We did open air meetings on the corner of King and Benton Street in Kitchener. Every week we would set up and play instruments and sing and preach the gospel. We saw many people come to Christ on that street corner.

Another evening, I went into an arcade and handed out gospel tracts. A young man at the back of the arcade was suicidal and didn't want to live anymore. When he saw us handing out tracts, he prayed, "God, if you really love me and care about me, I want you to get him to come and talk to me personally." Then he stood there and waited and watched.

That night, I didn't go to the back end of the arcade. I stayed at the front and never did talk to him. I left without giving him a tract. I had no idea that he had prayed that prayer.

About a month later, I got a phone call from a counselling centre saying that there was a young man there who had called in and was thinking about committing suicide. They were wondering if I could go over and talk to him immediately.

They gave me the address and I went over to his apartment building. When the door opened, a young man stood there, his life torn and full of all kinds of depression and problems. His eyes were filled with such hopelessness.

"Don't tell me about your God," he said. "I don't want to hear anything. A month ago, I was in an arcade and you were at the front passing out tracts. I asked God for you to come and talk to me personally, but you never did. You walked out the door."

"Did you ever think that out of three hundred thousand people in this region, God would pick me to come and talk to you here tonight?" I asked. "You see, He did answer your prayer. He brought me right to your house, even though I didn't talk to you in the arcade that night."

It had never dawned on him that his prayer was answered. He invited me in and I began to share Christ with him. He gave his life to Christ and I asked him to come and live with us for a few weeks until he got his life in order. He came to my mom's house, and we gave him a bedroom and food and lots of love. We ministered to him until we felt that his life was on the right track. God can do amazing things if only we believe.

For my first couple of years of being a Christian, I had an old 1968 Chevy. It was pretty much at the end of its life, but at least it still ran. I had no money to buy a new car and I felt that God didn't want me to go into debt because He was calling me into ministry. That old car took me all over Ontario and parts of the United States so I could keep ministering and preaching Jesus.

One night, the car was parked out in front of a church while I was inside during the evening service. All of a sudden, somebody came up to me and said, "Somebody just ran into your car out in front of the church." I went outside and saw that a lady had hit the side of my car and literally destroyed the vehicle. I thank God that she wasn't hurt, but my car was wrecked. Now I had no car and I had no money.

I went to the insurance company and they told me it was a write-off and they would give me $250. I began to argue rather than trust God. I phoned the insurance company over and over again, and I kept saying, "I need more money." After a couple of months, they finally said, "Okay, we will give you more money. We'll give you $300 and we'll let you keep the car."

At that point, I committed it to the Lord and believed that God would get me a good car for $300. Not long after, a young man in church came up to me and said that he had a car to sell. The car he owned was a beautiful car with a new paintjob, tinted windows, chrome wheels, and a beautiful interior with all the bells and whistles. It was worth thousands of dollars. It was just like new and he said that I had first crack at buying this vehicle. He told me to come over to his house that night and talk a deal. I prayed about it, took my $300, and went to his house.

He asked me how much I wanted to pay, and I asked him how much he wanted. He said he didn't know. He then said he would write out some prices on papers and put them in a hat. Whatever price I drew out of the hat, I could have the car for that amount. I began to pray in the Spirit, believing that God would help me to draw out the right price. When I pulled out the paper and opened it up, it said $300—the exact amount of money I had from the insurance company.

God shall supply all your need according to his riches in glory by Christ Jesus. (Philippians 4:19)

The Lord also opened doors for me to speak in prisons, high schools, youth rallies, and meetings in churches all over the country. My ministry began to unfold supernaturally as God directed me. I was studying at a Bible school at the time, preparing for God to take me into full-time ministry.

After seven years of studying, witnessing, doing street work, and running a youth centre, that day finally arrived. God released me to get married to my girlfriend Edith and begin my ministry. I had a good job running bulldozers building highways, but eventually I had to take a leap of faith and quit my job.

There are two things you need in life as a Christian. You need to know God's will and you need to know His timing for His will to come to pass. You can't have one without the other; they must work hand in hand. For seven years, I was in training, waiting upon the Lord, being mentored by the Holy Spirit. God was teaching me many things I needed to know for the future.

The first few years of my ministry were pretty tough and very lean. My wife and I had to live with my mother for a number of years so we could make ends meet. But David said, *"I have been young, and now am old; yet have I not seen the righteous forsaken, nor his seed begging bread"* (Psalm 37:25). God always put food on the table, gas in the car, and He always made sure we had enough.

God gave me a verse to encourage us in waiting on His timing and promises:

> *And therefore will the Lord wait, that he may be gracious unto you, and therefore will he be exalted, that he may have mercy upon you: for the Lord is a God of judgment: blessed are all they that wait for him.* (Isaiah 30:18)

Chapter 10

THE CALL

The Lord had put a call on my life right after I was saved. A few years later, He spoke to me about quitting my job and launching out into ministry. I believed that He would take care of me. When I entered full-time ministry, it was totally by faith. No paycheque and nobody supporting me.

God began to work in supernatural signs and wonders to touch people's lives. I watched drug addicts and criminals weep as I shared Jesus with them. Tears ran like a waterfall down their faces. I saw many hardened criminals come to Christ and have their lives turned around. Today they are productive young men and women, married with children and they hold down full-time jobs.

As long as you know it's the Lord leading you, you are safe to leap into the unknown. But you never want to go out into ministry on presumption. You've got to know that it is leading you and directing your life.

I felt that God wanted me to open a youth centre in downtown Kitchener. It was called Shilo Christian Youth Activity Centre. I ran that centre for quite a few years. On the weekends, we would have a hundred young people, sometimes more, jam into the youth centre. We brought in gospel groups and speakers and had Bible studies. We also had fun times with games and snacks while giving the young people hope for the future.

The Lord spoke to me that fifty percent of the young people coming to the centre were to be Christian. He then brought in the rest of the youth from the streets. Mixing Christian kids with people from the streets helped us maintain a good atmosphere. We ran it as a Christian youth centre, but we continually reached out to street kids to come and join us. It was located right in the core of Kitchener-Waterloo's east end. That was the toughest area of the city, where all the drug addicts, bikers, and prostitutes hung out.

After I opened the drop-in centre, I believed that God would pay the bills. As I heard one preacher say, "God's will is God's bill." At one point, I was $600 in debt and had no money to pay off the expenses to keep the centre open. I didn't tell anybody; I just prayed about it and asked God for help. I said, "Lord, if you want me to keep this street ministry going and keep this centre open, I need you to pay that $600 debt for me."

We had a little box by the doorway for people to donate. Some people would slip a couple of bucks into the box, but usually there was just garbage like gum wrappers, potato chip bags, etc. One day when I opened the box, I noticed that there were three pieces of paper wrapped up square with scotch tape. I opened one of them and found a $100 bill inside. I opened the second one and found another $100 bill. When I opened the third one, there was another $100 bill. There was no name, no phone number, and no way of knowing how that money got in there.

I showed it to my wife Edith, as I was really excited that God was beginning to answer my prayer. The next night, Edith opened up the box and saw three more pieces of paper wrapped in scotch tape. She called for me to come and look. We opened those wrapped pieces of paper only to find three more $100 bills. We received $600, right to the penny of what I'd asked God to provide. The next day, I went down to the mailbox. Inside was a letter with a cheque: a donation to the youth centre. When I looked at that cheque, the Lord spoke to me and said, "Your cup runs over. I always do more than you ask."

The Bible says, *"Now unto him that is able to do exceeding abundantly above all that we ask or think, according to the power that worketh in us..."* (Ephesians 3:20)

We had some very lean and hard years doing evangelism, trying to raise money and living in a small apartment at my mother's house. However, God was always faithful. He always met our needs and supplied everything necessary to keep me going in full-time ministry.

Over my years of ministry, I've travelled to many countries, including India, Egypt, Trinidad, Jamaica, Africa, Cuba, Haiti, and Sri Lanka. I've seen the Lord work many supernatural signs and wonders. These miracles are different from the natural realm, but they are still very real. I also went to Mexico a number of times. God opened my heart and spoke to me about going to that nation.

One night, when I was preaching in Tijuana, God performed one of the most amazing miracles. We were preaching outside and there were approximately four to five hundred people in attendance. Tijuana is a very dangerous place. Many police officers had been shot and police chiefs killed by the drug cartel. That night, I preached about how God can do anything. If anybody needs a healing or a miracle, God can give them a miracle.

A man came up when I began the altar call and said that he wanted to talk over the microphone. We allowed him to speak. He told the people that he had been born without one of his ears. When I looked at it him, I noticed only flat skin where there should have been an ear. He had no inner eardrum, no hole, literally no ear at all. To make matters worse, he was almost fully deaf in the other ear. He wanted a miracle and was asking God to put an ear on his head.

I suddenly realized that he had just told four hundred people that he wanted an ear. I thought to myself, *I'm better at cutting them off, like Peter in the garden of Gethsemane, than I am at putting them back on.* God's Word tells us that Peter cut off an ear, but Jesus picked it up and put it back on the high priest servant's head again and healed him.

"What am I to do with this situation?" I asked the Lord. The Lord told me just to pray and leave the rest with Him. I laid my hand on the man's head and began to pray for a miracle. I said, "Lord, this man wants an ear, and I pray in the name of Jesus Christ that you would grant his request and give him a miracle." It wasn't a long prayer, it wasn't a super spiritual prayer; it was just a simple prayer of faith. When I took my hand away from the side of his head, there was still no ear on his head. The Holy Spirit whispered into my heart the words of 2 Corinthians 5:7: "You walk not by sight but by faith."

I told him to go and thank God for the miracle, not really knowing what was happening. Some people might have thought that was just a copout because God didn't do anything. But I realized that if he was going to get a miracle, it was in God's hands, not mine.

The next night when I was preaching, the man came back. In the middle of the meeting, he came up and said he wanted to talk, so we gave him the microphone. He got up and said, "I was here last night and I told everyone that I was born deaf and I do not have an ear on this side of my head." He showed the assembly of people that there was only skin on the side of his face and no ear. "Last night, I asked God to give me an ear and to give me hearing for the first time in my life since I was born. After the man of God prayed for me, I went home. The telephone rang and I picked it up and all of a sudden I realized that I was listening on the phone with an ear that doesn't exist. I have perfect hearing on this side of my head and yet I don't have an ear."

The people began to praise the Lord. To me, that was a greater miracle than if God had put an ear on his head. God gave him perfect hearing without even having an ear.

After he testified, two young girls came up all dressed in black. They had black hair, black nail polish, and black lipstick. They wanted to speak on the microphone. The Holy Spirit prompted our hearts to let them share.

One of the girls grabbed the microphone and said, "We are witches. We serve Satan and we came here to curse everyone. We came to destroy your meeting and call in demon powers. Since we have seen the miracle of this man being healed and being able to hear without an ear, we have made a decision. Tonight we want to renounce Satanism and witchcraft and we want to give our lives to Jesus Christ."

What an amazing time we had that night as those two young girls surrendered their lives to Christ. In ministry, you have to be aware that you're wrestling not against flesh and blood but against principalities and powers and spiritual wickedness in high places (Ephesians 6:12). I have had demon-possessed people come to my house and I've seen God's power set them free.

One day I was sipping lemonade with two Christians in their backyard. A man unknown to us came into the yard and said that he was from England; he was stuck in Canada due to an airline strike. As he spoke, I felt a satanic presence. He then ignored the other two men and looked at me. He asked me what all this stuff was about salvation and God. He told me that he didn't need my God and that he wasn't afraid to die. At that point, his face literally disappeared and I was looking straight into the face of Lucifer, who said, "I have still got you, and you still belong to me."

At first I felt tremendous fear, but I heard the Holy Spirit tell me to just say, "Jesus!" When I said Jesus, he backed away.

I said it again and told the man that I wasn't afraid of him because I believed in Jesus. He turned and ran out of the yard.

What was really strange was the fact that the other two Christians saw the man but didn't hear and see the things I did. That's because I was locked in a supernatural battle with the devil. I had seen demonic things when doing drugs but thought they were only hallucinations. I realize now that there is a supernatural realm that we as Christians battle on a daily basis.

Behold, I give unto you power to tread on serpents and scorpions, and over all the power of the enemy: and nothing shall by any means hurt you. (Luke 10:19)

I have seen many miracles over the years. People have been healed from cancers and incurable terminal illnesses. One of our members at church, whose name is Harold, had a gangrene toe that went completely black. The doctor said that it had to be amputated. Harold came for prayer that week, believing God for a miracle. The next time the nurse saw him and took off the bandage, he had a brand new toe; the black shell of gangrene pulled off when the nurse gave a tug on the toe.

Our head usher, Madeline, was diagnosed with incurable cancer. It was already in her bones and the doctor said there was nothing he could do for her. Evangelist Franklin Walden came to our church and prayed for her healing at the altar call. She was instantly and totally healed, which was confirmed by doctors.

My cousin Brenda had a lump below her kidney that the doctors thought may be cancerous, or a sign of tuberculosis. I went to the hospital and prayed with her the night before surgery. During the prayer, she said the room filled up with a cloud and she felt like she was in a hot bath with warm water flowing over her body. She knew that she was healed, but the doctors didn't believe her. When they did surgery, they found that the lump had disappeared and there was an indentation where it had shown up on the x-rays.

Brenda's two daughters also both experienced miracles through prayer. Laura was born with a hole in her heart, and the doctors were very concerned. After prayer, the hole closed up by the power of God. Lindsay had an umbilical hernia at birth and was healed after her mom laid hands on her and prayed. Praise the Lord, nothing is too difficult for Jesus.

God also gave us a radio and TV ministry called Faith On Fire. It airs all across our nation on TV and around the world on the internet. To God be all the glory!

Chapter 11

THE MESSAGE

One of the major differences between Christianity and other world religions is that Jesus Christ proved who He was by rising from the dead after His crucifixion. Our own creator came down to die for us, and by His own power came back from the grave. Jesus said,

> *Therefore doth my Father love me, because I lay down my life, that I might take it again. No man taketh it from me, but I lay it down of myself. I have power to lay it down, and I have power to take it again. This commandment have I received of my Father.* (John 10:17–18)

The Bible also says, *"For God so loved the world, that he gave his only begotten Son, that whosoever believeth in him should not perish, but have everlasting life."* (John 3:16).

When Mary and Martha's brother Lazarus died, Martha said to Jesus, *"Lord, if thou hadst been there, my brother had not died"* (John 11:21). Jesus replied, *"I am the resurrection, and the life: he that believeth in me, though he were dead, yet shall he live: and whosoever liveth and believeth in me shall never die"* (John 11:25–26).

The second thing Christianity has that other world religions don't is a Saviour. In every other religion, you've got to try to earn God's favour by good works and obeying strict rules. Every man, woman, and child on the planet will fail in that area. No one can be good enough to please a Holy God.

Religion is man reaching up to God, but Jesus Christ is God reaching down to man. He came to do what we could not. We are saved when we believe on Him, that He died for our sins and that He rose from the dead. When we invite Him into our hearts, we become born again.

Jesus said, *"Except a man be born again, he cannot see the kingdom of God"* (John 3:3). He exchanges His righteousness for our sins and gives us a free gift of eternal life. Ephesians 2:8–9 tells us, *"For by grace are ye saved through faith; and that not of yourselves: it is the gift of God: not of works, lest any man should boast."*

Grace simply means undeserved favour, or if you spell it out:

G-R-A-C-E: God's righteousness at Christ's expense.
F-A-I-T-H: Forsaking all, I trust Him.
B-I-B-L-E: Blessed information bringing life eternal.

Salvation is a gift from God. Romans 6:23 says, *"For the wages of sin is death; but the gift of God is eternal life through Jesus Christ our Lord."* A gift is free and given because you love somebody. Wages are earned and you get paid at the end of the day. We have earned our place in hell, but God gave us a way out through believing on His son Jesus. Gifts are paid for by the one giving them, not the one receiving them. Jesus took the punishment for sin (the wages) so we could have mercy and go to heaven by grace alone. But you must accept a gift before it becomes yours! As one preacher said, "Jesus got what He didn't deserve so we could avoid what we do deserve."

Eternal life is gained only by faith in what Christ did for us, not what we do for Christ.

Ephesians 2:10 tells us that *"we are His workmanship, created in Christ Jesus unto good works."* It is the cart behind the horse. Good works cannot save us; they merely tell the world that there has been a change in our lives. When we become Christians, our fruits begin to prove that God has changed us from the inside out. He gave us a new heart.

> *Therefore if any man be in Christ, he is a new creature: old things are passed away; behold, all things are become new.* (2 Corinthians 5:17)

> *Now the just shall live by faith...* (Hebrews 10:38)

Today, if you desire to be a Christian, just pray this simple prayer from your heart:

> Lord Jesus, I know that I have sinned against You and I am sorry for what I have done. I believe that You died to save me from my sins and that You rose from the dead to give me eternal life. I am asking You to forgive me for all my sins and make me what You want me to be. I give You all my life and heart and I thank You for Your forgiveness in my life. In Jesus' name, amen.

Now that you have become a new Christian by faith, you need to find yourself a good Bible-teaching, spirit-filled church to grow spiritually with other believers. You also need to tell people that you are a Christian, as that will make you strong in the Lord.

> *That if thou shalt confess with thy mouth the Lord Jesus, and shalt believe in thine heart that God hath raised him from the dead, thou shalt be saved. For with the heart man believeth unto righteousness; and with the mouth confession is made unto salvation. For the scripture saith, Whosoever believeth on him shall not be ashamed.* (Romans 10:9–11)

I trust that I will see you in heaven one day, where we can spend time with our Lord and Saviour Jesus Christ!